Green Computing

Green Computing

Sustainability in Software

Rafeal Mechlore

Readers Publications

CONTENTS

INDEX 1

INTRODUCTION 3

1 | Chapter 1 13

2 | Chapter 2 33

3 | Chapter 3 52

4 | Chapter 4 77

5 | Chapter 5 97

6 | Chapter 6 119

7 | Chapter 7 139

8 | Chapter 8 165

INDEX

Introduction

1. Defining Green Computing
2. Significance of Green Computing in Software
3. Objectives of the Book

Chapter 1 :Environmental Impact of Software
1.1 The Carbon Footprint of Software
1.2 Energy Consumption and Efficiency
1.3 Electronic Waste and Sustainability

Chapter 2 :Energy-Efficient Software Development
2.1 Code Optimization for Reduced Energy Use
2.2 Green Algorithms and Their Application
2.3 Best Practices for Sustainable Software Design

Chapter 3 :Sustainable Data Centers and Infrastructure
3.1 Energy-Efficient Data Center Design
3.2 Leveraging Virtualization and Cloud for Green Computing
3.3 Integrating Renewable Energy in Data Centers

Chapter 4 :Extending Hardware Lifespan
4.1 Software's Role in Hardware Longevity
4.2 Repairability and Upgradability in Software Design
4.3 Circular Economy Approaches in Technology

Chapter 5 :Sustainable Software Development Practices
5.1 Embracing Eco-Conscious Design Principles
5.2 Environmental Impact Assessment in Software Projects

5.3 Cultivating a Culture of Sustainability

Chapter 6 :Challenges and Future Trends
6.1 Overcoming Barriers to Green Computing Adoption
6.2 Emerging Technologies and Future Prospects
6.3 Envisioning the Role of Green Computing

Chapter 7 :Tools, Resources, and Guidelines
7.1 Software Tools for Sustainable Development
7.2 Key Organizations and Initiatives in Green Computing
7.3 Practical Guidelines for Sustainable Software Practices

Chapter 8 :Conclusion and Call to Action
8.1 Recap of Key Takeaways
8.2 The Importance of Individual and Collective Action
8.3 The Role of Green Computing in a Sustainable Future

INTRODUCTION

In this digital age where things change quickly, information technology (IT) has become essential to all areas of life, including companies, governments, and our daily lives. Technology has made our lives easier, but it has also hurt the world in big ways. Concerns about the environment are growing because of the constant expansion of data centers, the wide availability of electronics, and the energy-intensive needs of software. Against this background, the idea of "Green Computing" has come up as a ray of light, providing a way to environmental sustainability in the IT field.

Green computing, which is also called sustainable computing or eco-friendly computing, changes how we think about, build, and run software systems and IT infrastructure. At its core, it is a promise to balance the unstoppable march of technical progress with the urgent need to leave less of an impact on the environment. This way of thinking acknowledges that the IT business, which has both caused and benefited from the digital revolution, needs to take care of the environment right away.

This introduction sets the stage for a deep look at Green Computing, which will look at its roots, guiding principles, and the key role it plays in making software development and IT processes less harmful to the environment.

How to Define "Green Computing"

Green computer is an idea that includes many different practices, strategies, and technologies that are all meant to make computer processes and infrastructure less harmful to the environment. It's basically about making software and IT processes more sustainable by trying to use less energy, resources, and make less electronic waste while also being as efficient as possible and putting out as little carbon as possible.

The idea behind Green Computing comes from the fact that the IT industry uses a lot of energy and releases a lot of carbon into the air. It was expected that data centers used about 1% of the world's electricity in 2019. This number keeps going up as our reliance on digital services grows. Also, making and throwing away electronic devices adds to the amount of electronic trash that builds up, which makes it very hard to recycle and get rid of.

The main goal of Green Computing is to find a balance between the many great things about technology and the need to take care of our world. In order to make IT more sustainable and eco-friendly, it tries to minimize its negative effects and increase its good effects on society.

The Need to Protect the Environment

People are becoming more aware of the environmental problems our world is facing, which is why Green Computing is needed. Some of the most important problems that need our help right now are climate change, species loss, resource depletion, and pollution. As we think about the effects of these problems, it becomes clearer that every business, including the IT one, needs to do something to reduce its impact on the environment.

Changes in the climate: Burning fossil fuels releases greenhouse gases, mostly carbon dioxide (CO_2). These gases warm the Earth's atmosphere and cause climate change. With its huge energy use, the IT industry adds to these emissions, which is why it is being targeted for efforts to cut emissions.

Resource Depletion: Too much effort is being put into taking out and using up limited natural resources, like rocks and rare metals used in electronics. Green computing tries to cut down on the use of resources and encourages sustainable buying.

Electronic Waste: Because technology changes so quickly, electronic gadgets become useless very quickly. This makes a lot of electronic trash, and a lot of it is thrown away in the wrong way or not recycled. Green Computing supports making devices last longer and encouraging people to recycle and properly throw away old electronics.

Energy Efficiency: Fossil fuels are often used to power data centers and other IT systems. To fight this, Green Computing stresses how important it is to use less energy and incorporate green energy sources.

Sustainability: Because people depend on technology more and more, the IT business needs to start using methods that are in line with larger goals for sustainability. The goal of green computing is to make IT operations and software creation more environmentally friendly.

What the book is trying to do

The goal of this book, "Green Computing: Sustainability in Software," is to be an all-around guide to the complicated world of Green Computing. It aims to shed light on the ideas, tactics, technologies, and best practices that support this very important field. We will look at different aspects of Green Computing over the course of several parts. This will give readers the information and tools they need to make environmentally friendly decisions when developing software and running IT businesses.

Education: To help readers fully grasp the idea of "Green Computing," how important it is, and how it fits into today's IT world.

To inform: To show the newest research, developments, and case studies in Green Computing, showing how companies are using sustainable methods in the real world.

Empower: To give IT experts, software developers, and people in charge of making decisions the information and useful tips they need to use Green Computing concepts in their work and support them.

Inspire: To get everyone in the IT business to commit to sustainability and build a culture of caring for the environment.

Challenges: To talk about the problems and issues that might come up when using green computing methods and give advice on how to solve them.

Anticipate the Future: To look into new technologies and trends in Green Computing that will help us understand what the future holds for environmentally friendly software development and IT operations.

Each of these goals will be looked at in more detail in the following parts, which will give you a full picture of Green Computing, from its basic ideas to its real-world uses. This book is for anyone who is interested in how technology and sustainability can work together, whether they are an IT professional, a software developer, a decision-maker in their company, or just someone who likes reading about these topics.

We will take a trip through the many facets of Green Computing in the following parts, looking at its different aspects, strategies, and real-life examples. We will look into the important part of making software that uses less energy, the design of sustainable data centers, ways to cut down on electronic waste, and the changes that need to happen in the way IT companies work in order for Green Computing to become standard practice.

We hope that by the end of this journey, you will not only have a deep understanding of how important Green Computing is, but also have the tools and information to use environmentally friendly methods in your own IT work.

Together, we can use technology to make the world a better place and make sure that future generations will have a more stable and eco-friendly world.

1. **Defining Green Computing**

    Green computing, which is also called sustainable computing or eco-friendly computing, is a broad idea that has become more popular recently as the IT industry tries to deal with the environmental problems that come with its fast growth. At its core, Green Computing is a promise to make sure that computer processes and systems have the least possible effect on the environment while also being as efficient and long-lasting as possible. This in-depth look will describe Green Computing, go into its history, look at its guiding principles, and talk about how it applies to today's world.
    The Start of Green Computing

In the late 20th century, when computers were first widely used and technology was rapidly improving, the idea of "Green Computing" was first put forward. People started to worry about the effects technology was having on the environment as it became more common in daily life and work.

One of the first signs of these worries was people becoming aware of how much energy machines use. In the 1990s, the U.S. Environmental Protection Agency (EPA) started the Energy Star program to find and support computers, monitors, and other electronics that use less energy. This project was a big step toward recognizing that computers have an effect on the world and that we need to do something about it.

As the IT industry grew over the next few years, people started talking more about electronic waste (e-waste), carbon emissions from data centers, and running out of resources. For these problems to be solved, it became clear that a broad method was needed, going beyond just saving energy. So, the idea of "Green Computing" began to take shape, which includes a wider range of environmental concerns.

How to Define "Green Computing"

Green computing means making computers, servers, and related parts like monitors, printers, and networking gear as environmentally friendly as possible when they are designed, built, used, and thrown away. It takes a whole-person view that looks at the whole lifecycle of IT goods and services, with the goal of using less energy, throwing away less electronics, and using environmentally friendly methods.

Some important parts of the meaning of "green computing" are:

Energy Efficiency: Hardware and apps that use less energy are very important for green computing. To do this, computer systems need to be made to use less power while they're running, and data centers need to take steps to save energy.

Resource conservation: It encourages the smart use of metals, minerals, water, and other natural resources in the making of IT tools. This includes using environmentally friendly ways to get things and starting recycling programs.

Electronic Waste Reduction: To cut down on e-waste, Green Computing tries to make electronics last longer, make them easier to fix, and make it easier to properly dispose of and recycle electronics.

Clean Energy: One of the main ideas behind Green Computing is to power data centers and IT processes with clean energy sources like solar or wind power.

Sustainable Software: It supports eco-friendly practices and encourages the creation of software that is optimized for speed, uses less energy, and is more sustainable.

Lifecycle Thinking: Green Computing uses a "cradle-to-grave" method to look at how IT products and services affect the environment at all stages, from making them to throwing them away.

How to Do Green Computing

Energy Efficiency: Making sure that IT tools and infrastructure use as little energy as possible so that less carbon is released into the air.

Virtualization: Using virtualization technologies to combine real servers into one, make better use of resources, and cut down on the need for extra hardware.

Cloud computing means using cloud services to change the size of resources on the fly, which cuts down on the need for equipment on-site and encourages sharing of resources.

Renewable energy means running data centers and other IT buildings with energy from renewable sources like solar and wind power instead of fossil fuels.

Lifecycle Management: Making sure that IT equipment is properly disposed of at the end of its useful life by recycling, refurbishing, or reusing it so that as little e-waste as possible is produced.

Sustainable Procurement: Buying IT goods and services from companies that care about the environment and practice sustainable sources.

Software optimization means making and using software that works better and uses less energy.

Eco-Friendly Design: Making IT goods with the environment in mind, such as choosing eco-friendly materials, energy-efficient parts, and products that can be recycled.

Cultural awareness means creating a culture of sustainability in IT companies and encouraging workers to make decisions that are good for the environment.

Why green computing is important now

Energy Use: Data centers and IT systems are using more and more energy. It is thought that data centers alone use more than 1% of the world's electricity. Green computing provides ways to reduce this need for energy.

Concerning climate change, the IT industry adds to carbon emissions by using a lot of energy and making electrical goods. In the fight against climate change, reducing these pollutants is very important.

Resource Scarcity: In order to make electronics, limited natural materials must be taken out of the ground. Green computing tries to cut down on the use of resources and encourage environmentally friendly habits.

E-Waste: Getting rid of electronic waste is bad for the earth. Green Computing supports making devices last longer and properly handling electronic trash.

Sustainability Goals: A lot of businesses and governments are making sustainability goals, which can include carbon neutrality aims. These goals are in line with green computing.

Cost Savings: Green practices like using less energy and resources wisely not only help the world but also save people and businesses money.

Standards and regulations: Rules and regulations for being environmentally responsible are getting more attention. IT companies must follow these rules at all times.

Public Awareness: People are becoming more aware of environmental issues, and this includes both customers and workers. Companies that put ecology first can get ahead of the competition and improve their image.

2. **Significance of Green Computing in Software**

People don't always think about how software development affects the environment because we live in a world that is becoming more and more digital and where technology is everywhere. But it's impossible to stress how important green computing is in software. It's an important and creative way to get the IT business to use less carbon and be more environmentally friendly. This article will go into great detail about how important green computing is in software, looking at its effects on the environment, the economy, and society.

1. **Importance for the environment**
   How to Save Energy
   One of the main environmental benefits of green computing in software is that it can make use of energy more efficiently. It is well known that traditional data centers and computer systems use a lot of energy. But as more energy-efficient algorithms, virtualization technologies, and improved code are made, software can make a big difference in lowering the amount of energy used by data centers and personal computers. We can slow down climate change and lower greenhouse gas pollution by making software programs use less power.
   Keeping resources safe
   Green computing is also a key part of protecting important environmental resources. Electronic waste (e-waste) is a big problem for the earth because of how electronic devices are made and thrown away. Making software that makes hardware last longer and changes that use fewer resources can help lower the need for new devices, which in turn lowers e-waste.
   Using the cloud
   Cloud computing has changed the IT industry by giving companies the ability to grow and change as needed. But data centers that power cloud services are known for using a lot of electricity. Software that uses green computing can make the best use of cloud resources, making sure that data centers work as efficiently as possible while also having less of an effect on the environment.
2. **Importance for Business**
   Cutting costs
   Businesses and people can save a lot of money by using green computing in software. Companies can lower their energy bills, lower the cost of maintaining

their hardware, and make their IT systems last longer by optimizing code and using energy-efficient methods. These cost cuts can make the bottom line a lot better in the long run.

An edge over the competition

More and more people are worried about the environment, and investors and customers are drawn to businesses that put sustainability first. Businesses that use green computing not only help the world but also get an edge over their competitors. They can advertise their goods and services as being good for the environment, which will bring in customers and investors who care about the environment and want to support sustainable projects.

Compliance with Regulations

The rules that governments around the world have on protecting the environment are getting tighter. Businesses can make sure they follow these rules and avoid fines and legal problems by using green computer practices. Taking this proactive approach to sustainability can protect the image and financial health of a business.

3. **Importance in society**

Learning and Being Aware

The use of green computing in software can be used to teach people about environmental problems. When IT and software writers add energy-saving features to their work, they send a strong message to users about how important it is to be environmentally friendly. These learning opportunities can motivate people and groups to live more environmentally friendly lives.

Making jobs

The move to "green" computing is creating jobs in many fields, from renewable energy to software creation. As the need for software and tools that use less energy grows, so does the need for skilled workers in these areas. This could help the economy grow and lower unemployment.

Global Working Together

Green computing is an international project that goes beyond borders. International groups, countries, and people are encouraged to work together to solve environmental problems. Sharing the best green computing methods and information makes it easier for people around the world to work together to fight climate change.

It's impossible to say enough about how important green computing is in software. It is an important part of a sustainable future because it is good for the earth, the economy, and society. Green computing not only lowers the IT industry's carbon impact, but it also helps make the world more sustainable and prosperous by encouraging people to use less energy, save resources, cut costs, and care about the environment. As more software developers and IT professionals follow green computing principles, we get closer to a world where technology and sustainability live together in peace, which is good for everyone.

C. Objectives of the Book

Every book has goals, which are either stated directly or weaved into the story in a subtle way. These goals help the author write a story that makes sense and has meaning, and they also let readers know what to expect from the book. This essay will talk about the idea of aims in literature and the different goals that authors may have when they write a book, such as teaching, entertaining, inspiring, and challenging.

1. **Giving the Reader Knowledge**

   One of the main goals of many books is to teach the reader something. There are many types of educational books, such as textbooks, academic papers, and non-fiction books that try to teach readers about a certain field. The goal of these books is to teach, clarify, and increase the reader's knowledge about the topic.

   Content that is useful

   Books that are meant to teach usually include facts, historical background, science principles, or expert opinions. Their goal is to make the person smarter and more knowledgeable about a certain topic. For instance, the goal of a science guidebook might be to teach students about the basics of physics, while the goal of a history book might be to teach readers about a certain time period.

   Getting Better Skills

   Some books are written to help people learn new skills or get better at ones they already have. This could include books with instructions on how to do things like cook, build things out of wood, or learn a language. This article's goal is to give people useful information and skills.

   Getting people to think critically

   Reading educational books might also help you think more deeply and develop your mind. Their ideas, arguments, or theories may be hard to understand, pushing readers to actively connect with the material and improve their analytical skills.

2. **Making the reader happy**

   Another common goal in writing is to entertain. Entertainment books are meant to entertain and keep readers interested, but they can also have important lessons and themes.

   Telling stories and telling stories

   Fictional books, short stories, and poems often try to entertain readers by telling interesting stories in vivid detail. These books take readers to different places, into the lives of the people, and make them feel a lot of different things.

   Fun and satire

   Satire and humor are big parts of some books that are meant to be fun. The point of these works is to make people laugh, think about problems in society, or make fun of everyday life.

Get away

It's possible that entertainment books are also a way for people to briefly escape the stresses and problems in their own lives. They give people a chance to relax and clear their minds.

3. **Motivating and inspiring people**

   Some books are meant to inspire and drive readers by telling personal stories, success stories, or examples of people who have been strong and kept going even when things got hard. These goals are all related to human growth and giving people more power.

   Changes in Person

   The point of books about personal growth is to motivate readers to become the best versions of themselves. They often give advice, tactics, and insights on things like how to improve yourself, how to be a better leader, and how to reach your goals.

   Getting Through Problems

   Biographies and autobiographies of people who have solved big problems in their lives can give people hope as they face their own problems. These books give people hope, strength, and the drive to keep going even when things get hard.

   How Things Change

   Some books try to get people to work together and make changes in society. They talk about things like human rights, social justice, and protecting the environment so that readers will want to work for good change in the world.

4. **Making you think and challenging you**

Books that are meant to challenge and spark thinking often deal with controversial or interesting ideas that make readers think about their own beliefs and assumptions.

Philosophical Study

Philosophical texts and essays are examples of writing that tries to make readers think by addressing difficult and general ideas. These works make you think deeply about yourself and have thoughtful conversations.

Thoughts on Society

Authors can criticize social norms, beliefs, and institutions through their works. The point of these books is to make people think and talk about important social problems and to get people to see things from different points of view.

Problems of morals

Some books put readers in moral and ethical situations where they have to make tough choices and question their own sense of right and wrong. The goal is to get people to think about and argue about moral issues.

There is a wide range of goals that a book can have, including teaching, entertaining, motivating, and making you think. The purpose and message an author wants to send to their readers help them choose their goals. Knowing the goals of a book can help readers get more out of it, make sure their hopes are realistic, and understand the author's point. Whether the goal of a book is to teach, entertain, inspire, or question, those goals shape the experience of the reader and the effect it has on their lives.

Chapter 1

Environmental Impact of Software

Software is now an important part of everyday life in a world that is becoming more and more digital. It gives our devices power, keeps our info safe, and makes it easier to talk to each other and do business. Software has changed the way we live and work, but it also has a big effect on the world that people don't always think about. This thorough study looks into many aspects of how software affects the environment, including how much energy it uses, electronic waste, sustainable development, and ways to make the software business more eco-friendly.

1. **How much energy is used**

   Places to store data and servers
   The amount of energy that data centers and servers use is one of the biggest ways that software hurts the world. The hardware that runs software programs, websites, and cloud services is kept in these buildings. With the growth of cloud computing and the internet, the need for data centers has grown by a huge amount.

1. **The amount of energy used**
   Data centers are notorious for using a lot of electricity. Because they need to be cooled all the time, they use a lot of power. Server farms that support famous websites and social networks also run all the time, which makes them use even more electricity.
2. **Clean Energy Sources**

Some data centers are switching to clean energy sources like wind and solar power to lessen this effect. Their carbon output will go down, and this change will help them reach their sustainability goals.

Improvements to software

Software writers are very important for lowering energy use. Software can run faster on servers and end-user devices by making code more efficient and coming up with methods that use less energy. This optimization cuts down on wasted energy and greenhouse gas pollution.

1. **Programming languages that use less energy**
   One important way to lower software's impact on the world is to use programming languages and frameworks that use less energy. Some programs, like Go and Rust, are known for being quick, while others aren't as well known for that. Best techniques and tools for making software can also help with this.
2. **Containerization and virtualization**

Virtualization technologies, such as virtual machines and containers, make better use of computer resources. They let several software programs run on a single server, which cuts down on the number of actual machines needed and, in turn, the amount of energy used.

II. E-waste, or electronic waste

Getting rid of electronic trash, or e-waste, is another big environmental problem that comes with software. As technology changes quickly, many gadgets become useless, which means that a lot of electronics have to be thrown away.

Plans for Obsolescence

Updates and new versions of software are sometimes meant to get people to buy new gear. This method, called "planned obsolescence," adds to e-waste by making older electronics less useful or suitable.

Designing Hardware That Will Last

Hardware companies are focused more and more on sustainable design principles to cut down on e-waste. Some ways to make hardware dumping less harmful to the environment are to use modular devices, parts that can be fixed, and responsible recycling programs.

III. Practices for sustainable development

Development of green software

The goal of green software creation is to make sure that the software is sustainable at all stages of its lifecycle. It takes the surroundings into account during the planning, writing, testing, launching, and upkeep stages.

1. **Assessment of the whole life cycle**

   LCA is a way to figure out how software affects the world over the course of its life. It takes things like emissions, energy use, and material use into account. Developers can find ways to make things better and make decisions that are better for the environment by doing LCAs.

2. **Review and cleanup of code**

Code reviews and optimization practices that are done on a regular basis help find and get rid of flaws that waste energy and resources. These changes are good for the environment and make apps run better.

Hardware that uses less energy

Even though software is a big part of how much energy something uses, hardware is also very important. Hardware that uses less energy, like processors, storage devices, and sensors, can make devices that run software use a lot less energy total.

1. **Certificate from Energy Star**
   Energy Star certification is a way to find gear and electronics that use less energy. Companies that follow the Energy Star guidelines make goods that use less electricity when they are running and when they are not in use.
2. **Adding hardware that uses less energy**

For lowering energy use, it is important to build products and data centers with hardware that uses less energy. Hardware design improvements continue to open up ways to make things run more smoothly.

IV. Web hosting and cloud computing

The way software services are provided and managed has changed a lot because of cloud computing. It allows for growth and adaptability, but it also has effects on the surroundings.

Virtualizing servers

Technologies for server virtualization, like virtual machines and containers, let more than one program run on the same hardware. By combining computers, we need fewer of them, which saves energy and leaves a smaller carbon footprint.

Where the data center is

If you look at where data centers are located, you can see how they affect the environment. Putting data centers in places that have access to clean energy sources like hydropower or wind power can cut their carbon output by a lot.

V. SaaS (Software as a Service) and Going Green

Software as a Service (SaaS) is becoming more and more popular because it is easy to use and doesn't cost much. However, it also affects how much energy is used.

Combining servers

Most of the time, SaaS companies pool their servers' resources to serve more than one client. This can save energy compared to separate businesses hosting their own servers.

How Well Users' Devices Work

Users' gadgets connect to SaaS apps that are hosted on remote servers. Making user devices, like laptops and smartphones, more energy-efficient can further lower the damage that SaaS use does to the world.

VI. Initiatives for rules and regulations

Governments and regulatory groups are becoming more aware of how software affects the environment and are taking steps to fix the problem.

The Ecodesign Directive

The Ecodesign Directive in the European Union says that energy-related goods, like software, must meet certain environmental standards. This directive pushes software and hardware designers to make things that use less energy.

The Energy Star Program

In the US, the Energy Star program certifies goods that use less energy, such as software. By taking part in the program, software developers and organizations can support software solutions that use less energy.

VII. Trends and Solutions for the Future

As people learn more about how software affects the world, a number of new trends and solutions are starting to appear.

Long-Term Software Certification

A sustainable software rating could help people and businesses find and choose software that has little to no effect on the environment, similar to the Energy Star program.

Using renewable energy sources

In the coming years, more and more data centers and server farms will likely use green energy sources. With this change, software systems will leave even less of a carbon footprint.

Data centers that last

To cut down on energy use, people who run data centers are looking into new ways to cool their buildings, like using liquid cooling. Also, data centers are being built with energy economy in mind more and more.

Principles of the Circular Economy

Adopting circular economy principles, which stress repair, reuse, and recycling, can help lessen the damage caused by electronic waste from old devices.

There are many things to think about when looking at how software affects the world, such as energy use, electronic waste, sustainable development, and more. It is important for people, groups, and politicians to understand how serious this effect is and take steps to lessen it.

The software industry can help make the future more sustainable by using less energy, writing better code, supporting environmentally friendly hardware design, and following green software development standards. Regulatory efforts, certification programs, and the use of green energy sources will also be very important in lowering the environmental impact of software.

Even though technology is always getting better, the software industry needs to keep working to reduce the damage it does to the environment. This way, the benefits of digital progress don't hurt the health of our world.

1.1 The Carbon Footprint of Software

Software is an important part of our lives now that we live in a digital world. It helps us communicate, makes tasks easier, and gives us fun. But the growing use of software has an environmental cost that isn't always thought about: its carbon effect.

This essay looks at the carbon footprint of software by looking at its different parts, how they affect the world, and what can be done to lessen that effect.

1. Getting to Know Software's Carbon Footprint
   How to Define Carbon Footprint

The amount of greenhouse gas pollution, mostly carbon dioxide (CO_2), that come from making, using, and distributing software is called its "carbon footprint." This footprint includes both direct and indirect emissions. Direct emissions come from things like the energy that servers and data centers use, while indirect emissions come from things like making hardware and electrical waste (e-waste).

Assessment of the whole life cycle

To figure out how much carbon software leaves behind, you need to do a full Life Cycle Assessment (LCA) that looks at emissions at all of its stages, from creation and deployment to disposal. This LCA method gives a full picture of the environmental effect.

2. **The Different Parts of the Carbon Footprint**

Phase of Development

1. **Need for Energy**
   Software creation takes work because you have to code, test, and fix bugs. Tasks that use a lot of energy, like compiling code or running simulations, add to the carbon impact.
2. **Making hardware**

During the software creation process, developers use computers and other tools. The carbon footprint of the software is increased by the emissions made when these gadgets are made.

Setting up and using

1. **Servers and data centers**
   Data centers use a lot of energy to cool and run their computers, which are where software is often stored. Emissions are affected by the hosting service, where the computer is located, and how well it works.
2. **Devices for End Users**

Smartphones, computers, and other devices that run apps need electricity to work. The carbon footprint of these gadgets can be changed by the source of energy used to charge them.

Electronic waste

Electronic garbage includes old software and hardware that can release harmful chemicals into the environment if it is not thrown away properly or recycled. Getting rid of more electronic waste is important for lowering software's carbon footprint.

III. Effects on the environment

Putting out greenhouse gases

The main damage that software's carbon footprint does to the world is by releasing greenhouse gases, mostly CO_2. Climate change and global warming are made worse by emissions from data centers, server farms, and development processes that use a lot of energy.

How much energy is used

A big part of the carbon impact is the energy that is needed to run data centers, servers, and end-user devices. It puts a strain on energy supplies and, when made from fossil fuels, makes environmental damage worse.

Running out of resources

Natural resources are used up when hardware devices are made, including those used for software creation and by end users. This destroys habitats and upsets ecosystems.

Pollution from E-Waste

Getting rid of e-waste the wrong way can hurt the environment. Electronic parts contain harmful chemicals that can pollute the water and dirt, which is bad for both people and plants.

IV. Getting software to leave less of a carbon footprint

How to Save Energy

1. **Improving the Data Center**

    One important way to cut down on carbon emissions is to make data centers more energy efficient. Some strategies are using cooling systems that work well, virtualizing servers, and getting power from green sources.

2. **Hardware that will last**

Choosing hardware that uses less energy for software creation and devices for end users can cut down on energy use and pollution. One way to support sustainability is to get people to use products that are Energy Star-certified.

Development of green software

1. **The optimization of code**
   Efficient coding and code optimization can lower the amount of energy that is used when software is running. This includes cutting down on computational jobs and resource use that aren't needed.
2. **Containerization and virtualization**
   By using virtualization and containerization technologies, software deployment can be made more efficient, which means that fewer physical computers are needed.
3. **Algorithms that last**

Most of the time, developing and using algorithms that use less energy can lead to big savings, especially in apps that use a lot of resources.

Renewable Power

1. **Getting Power**
   The carbon footprint of software infrastructure can be cut down by a lot by switching to green energy sources like solar, wind, and hydropower for data centers and server farms.
2. **Offsetting carbon emissions**

Another way for software companies to make up for their pollution is to buy carbon offsets.

These offsets help projects that cut down on or collect emissions in other places.

Designing Hardware That Will Last

1. **Design in Modules**
   Modular hardware makes it easier to fix problems and add new parts, which extends the life of gadgets and cuts down on e-waste.
2. **Reusing and recycling and proper disposal**

It is better for the earth if people are encouraged to recycle their old electronics through take-back programs or certified e-waste recycling facilities.

Eco-friendly ways to build things

1. **Work from home**
   Software companies can lower their carbon footprint by encouraging people to work from home. This will cut down on the energy used for getting to work.
2. **Offices that use less energy**

Companies that make software can make their offices more energy-efficient by adding things like LED lights and HVAC systems that use less energy.

A Supply Chain That Lasts

1. **Using ethical sources**
   Making sure that materials used to make hardware are gathered in an ethical way lowers the damage that getting and processing resources does to the world.
2. **The Ideas Behind the Circular Economy**

Adopting circular economy principles, which stress repair, reuse, and recycling, can make tools last longer and cut down on the need for new production.

V. The Part of Rules and Policies
The Ecodesign Directive

The European Union's Ecodesign Directive says that energy-related goods, like software, must meet certain environmental standards. It supports the creation of software and hardware that uses less energy.

The Energy Star Program

In the US, the Energy Star program certifies goods that use less energy, such as software. By taking part in the program, you help push software solutions that last.

Software's carbon footprint is a complicated and multifaceted problem that covers many stages of its lifecycle, from development and deployment to use and disposal. It adds to the pollution caused by greenhouse gases, energy use, resource loss, and e-waste.

Software developers, hardware makers, data center operators, policymakers, and users all need to work together to reduce the damage that software does to the world. To lower the carbon impact, things like using less energy, making software that is better for the environment, using renewable energy, and making hardware that lasts must be done.

The Ecodesign Directive and the Energy Star program are two important rules and guidelines that help the software business be more environmentally friendly. More and more people are becoming aware of how software affects the environment. Stakeholders need to take action to make sure that new software development leads to a more safe and eco-friendly future.

1.2 Energy Consumption and Efficiency

These days, energy use and efficiency are very important issues because of rising energy needs and environmental worries. As we move toward more safe energy sources and become more aware of climate change, it has never been more important to understand how much energy we use and how to make it as efficient as possible. This essay talks about energy usage and efficiency, what they mean, the problems they cause, and the steps we can take to make the future more sustainable.

1. **Energy Usage: The Present Situation**
   More people want to buy energy
   The world's need for energy keeps going up because of more people living in cities and better technology. Our energy infrastructure and resources are under more stress because of this higher demand, which raises worries about energy security and sustainability.
   How fossil fuels play a part
   Fossil fuels, such as coal, oil, and natural gas, have long been the world's main energy sources. However, their use has big effects on the environment, mostly in the form of air pollution and greenhouse gas releases.
   Effects on the Environment
   A big cause of climate change is using a lot of energy, especially energy that comes from fossil fuels. Burning fossil fuels releases greenhouse gases like carbon dioxide (CO_2) and methane (CH_4) into the air. These gases warm the Earth and cause other problems in the environment.
2. **Energy Efficiency: A Way to Make Things Last**

   How to Define Energy Efficiency
   Energy efficiency means using energy resources in the best way possible to get what you want while reducing waste and inefficiency as much as possible. It is one of the most important ideas in the quest for survival.
   Why energy efficiency is important

   1. **Benefits for the environment:** using less energy and putting out fewer greenhouse gases.

2. **Economic Benefits:** People, companies, and governments will save money on energy costs.
3. **Energy security:** relying less on fossil fuels that are running out.
4. **Technological Innovation:** Creating energy systems that are cleaner and use less energy.

III. Problems with Using Less Energy
Problems with technology

Implementing technologies and habits that use less energy is often slowed down by technical issues like high start-up costs and the need to improve infrastructure. Getting past these problems will take money and new ideas.

Behavior and Being Aware

How people act and how aware they are are very important for saving energy. Energy-saving attempts can be slowed down by not being aware of the problem, not wanting to change, or having bad habits.

Rules and policies

Policies and rules that aren't clear or aren't acceptable can slow down progress in energy efficiency. Businesses and people need to be encouraged to use less energy by having rules and incentives that work.

IV. Ways to Save Energy
Technologies that use less energy

1. When it comes to lighting, LED and CFL bulbs use less energy than regular incandescent lamps.
2. **Appliances:** Appliances with the Energy Star label use less electricity.
3. **HVAC Systems:** In modern homes, heating, ventilation, and air conditioning systems are made to use less energy.
4. **Transportation:** Electric cars and hybrid cars use less gas and put out fewer greenhouse gases.

Making Things Work Better

1. **Insulation:** Good insulation lowers the amount of energy needed for warmth and cooling.
2. **Technologies for smart buildings:** Automated systems and monitors help buildings use energy more efficiently.
3. **Passive Design:** This type of architectural design makes the most of natural light and air flow, so artificial lighting and HVAC systems are not needed as much.

Efficiency in Industry and Manufacturing

1. **Process Optimization:** To use less energy, industrial processes can be made better.
2. **Combined Heat and Power (CHP):** CHP devices take in waste heat and use it again, which makes the whole system more energy efficient.
3. **Energy Management Systems:** Modern systems keep an eye on and manage how much energy factories use.

Sources of renewable energy

1. **Solar Panels:** Photovoltaic systems use light to make power.
2. **Wind turbines:** Wind energy uses the wind's power to make electricity.
3. **Hydropower:** Dams that use moving water to make electricity are called hydroelectric dams.

Transportation that uses less energy

1. **Public Transit:** Public transportation methods that work well cut down on the energy use of individual cars.
2. **Carpooling and ridesharing:** Using shared transportation cuts down on pollution and fuel use.

3. **Walking and biking:** These non-motorized forms of transportation use less energy and are better for the earth.

Conservation and Management of Energy

1. **Energy Audits:** Auditing energy use shows you where you can make it better.
2. Behavior change programs teach people how to save energy by changing the way they do things.
3. **Buying green energy:** To make up for their carbon emissions, businesses can buy renewable energy credits.

Policies and incentives that last

1. **Carbon Pricing:** Putting in place carbon taxes or cap-and-trade systems makes people more likely to cut down on their emissions.
2. **Energy Efficiency Standards:** Making rules for how energy-efficient products and cars must be and making sure they are followed.
3. **Incentives for green Energy:** Giving tax breaks and money to people who use green energy.

VI. How renewable energy can help save energy
Change to clean energy

One important way to save energy and cut down on greenhouse gas pollution is to switch to renewable energy sources. Renewable energy methods are an alternative to fossil fuels that is long-lasting and low in carbon emissions.

Working together with saving energy

Using less energy and renewable energy are two methods that work well together. Energy efficiency steps lower the total amount of energy that is needed, which makes it easier to get that energy from renewable sources.

Energy Production in Different Places

Decentralized energy creation is possible with renewable energy sources like solar panels and wind turbines. This lowers the losses that come with centralized power plants during transfer and distribution.

VI. Why individual and group action are important

Each Person Is Responsible

The best way for individuals to help save energy is to adopt sustainable habits in their daily lives, like using less energy, saving water, and making smart buying choices.

Taking Action Together

For real progress to be made in energy efficiency and sustainability, people must work together through community projects, business sustainability programs, and government policies.

How we deal with environmental problems and climate change depends a lot on how much energy we use and how efficiently we use it. To make the future more sustainable, we need to understand how the energy we use affects other things, make technology and lifestyle changes that make us more efficient, and switch to green energy sources. Energy security and protecting the environment are very important problems that need to be dealt with by everyone, including individuals, businesses, and governments. By using less energy, we can make the world more stable and long-lasting for people now and in the future.

1.3 Electronic Waste and Sustainability

In a world that is becoming more and more digital, electronic gadgets are everywhere. They make our lives easier and connect us to others. Electronic waste, or e-waste, is a major environmental problem that has come up because of how quickly gadgets are becoming popular. This essay talks about the idea of electronic waste, how it affects the world, the problems it causes, and long-term ways to deal with this growing problem.

1. What Electronic Waste Is

What Is Electronic Waste (E-Waste)?

E-waste, which stands for "electronic waste," is made up of old or broken electronic gadgets and equipment. Smartphones, laptops, desktop computers, TVs, freezers, washing machines, and other electronics can be on this list. E-waste can be broken, old, or just useless electronics.

Different Types of E-Waste

1. **Consumer electronics:** This group includes things like smartphones, computers, and TVs that people use for personal or home use.
2. E-waste that is made up of computers, servers, printers, and networking gear used in business and industry is called information technology (IT) equipment.

II. The Effects of E-Waste on the Environment

Parts That Are Toxic

Heavy metals like lead, mercury, and cadmium, as well as flame retardants, are found in a lot of electronic products. If these toxins are thrown away in the wrong way, they can get into the environment and pollute land and water.

How much energy and resources are used

An enormous amount of energy and natural materials are needed to make electronics. Getting rare minerals out of the ground, making parts, and putting together gadgets all use energy and resources.

Footprint of Carbon

In more than one way, e-waste adds to carbon pollution. When fossil fuels are used, carbon gases are released during the making, transporting, and throwing away of electronics.

Dump Sites and Room

If you don't properly get rid of your e-waste, electronic gadgets can end up in landfills. This not only takes up valuable room, but it could also harm the environment by letting toxic substances leak out.

III. How E-Waste Is Getting Worse

Rapid progress in technology

Because technology changes so quickly, product lifecycles get shorter, which means that gadgets become useless more quickly. Because of this cycle of fast innovation, gadgets that are still working are often thrown away.

Proliferation of Electronic Devices

Electronic gadgets are becoming more popular because they are getting easier and cheaper to get. The amount of electronic waste keeps going up because more gadgets are being used.

Recycling and Dumping Without Permits

In some places, people recycle electronics informally or, even worse, dump them in places where they aren't supposed to be. When these things happen, they can pollute the environment, put workers' health at risk, and stop resources from being recovered.

IV. How to Handle E-Waste in a Sustainable Way
Extra Responsibility of the Producer

1. **EPR Laws:** Governments can pass EPR laws that make electronics companies responsible for collecting and recycling their own goods when they reach the end of their useful life.
2. **Eco-Design:** Companies can make goods using eco-friendly materials and parts that are easy to take apart, which makes recycling easier and cuts down on harmful parts.

Collection and recycling the right way

1. **Collection Programs:** Making it easy for people to drop off their electronic waste and set up collection programs urges them to do so responsibly.
2. **Certified Recycling Centers:** These places are licensed to safety take out valuable materials and get rid of dangerous ones.

Reusing and recycling materials

1. **Resource Extraction:** Gold, silver, and copper can be recovered from old electronics through recycling, which cuts down on the need to get new resources.
2. **Techniques that are good for the environment:** New ways of recycling, like hydrometallurgical processes, take less damage to the environment.

Principles of the Circular Economy

1. **Repair and Refurbishment:** Encouraging people to fix and refurbish devices increases the useful life of products and lowers the amount of electronic trash that is made.
2. **Reuse and Second-Hand Markets:** Reuse of electronics is encouraged by resale markets and donation programs, which lowers the need for new goods.

Being aware and learning

1. **Consumer Awareness:** Teaching people about how e-waste affects the world and how to properly get rid of it encourages them to act responsibly.
2. **School Programs:** Teaching students about e-waste as part of their regular lessons can help shape their future environmentally friendly habits.

Working Together Internationally

1. **Basel Convention:** The Basel Convention on the Control of Transboundary Movements of Hazardous Wastes and Their Disposal aims to set rules for the trade of hazardous waste, such as electronic waste.

2. **Agreements and Partnerships:** To solve the global e-waste problem, governments, NGOs, and the business sector must work together and sign international agreements.

V. New Ways to Recycle E-Waste

Mining in cities

Urban mining is the process of getting important metals and minerals out of trash in cities. This method cuts down on the need for traditional mining and the damage it does to the earth.

Following e-waste

Blockchain technology is being used to keep track of e-waste at all times, making sure it is recycled properly and cutting down on illegal dumping.

Recycling by Machine

Robotic systems and artificial intelligence are making the recycling of electronic trash safer and more efficient.

Electronic waste is becoming a bigger problem for the earth because of how quickly technology is changing, how many devices are being made, and how poorly they are thrown away. E-waste is bad for the climate, people's health, and the long-term use of resources.

For e-waste management to be sustainable, governments, manufacturers, consumers, and the recycling business all need to work together. For a complete solution to work, producers must take on more responsibility, make sure trash is properly collected and recycled, recover materials, follow the principles of the circular economy, educate and raise knowledge, and work together with other countries.

Getting rid of e-waste is not only the right thing to do for the earth, but it's also the first step toward a more sustainable and resource-efficient future. We can protect the health of our world for future generations by using eco-friendly methods and new recycling technologies to reduce the damage that electronic waste does to the environment.

Chapter 2

Energy-Efficient Software Development

The need for software programs and systems keeps growing at an amazing rate in a world that is becoming more and more digital. Software is an important part of almost every part of our lives, from phones and computers to data centers and the Internet of Things (IoT). But this fast growth in software creation has unintended effects, like using a lot of energy and having a negative effect on the environment. As the world struggles with climate change and running out of resources, it's important for the software development industry to adopt practices that use less energy.

This piece goes into detail about the idea of energy-efficient software development, looking at what it means, how it works, and some useful tips. We will talk about why energy efficiency is important, how software that isn't energy-efficient hurts the world, and how developers can help by using green computing methods.

Why energy-efficient software development is important

1. **Effects on the environment:**
   The amount of energy used by the IT business, which includes

making software, has been steadily going up. It is well known that data centers, which house and run computers that run software programs, use a lot of electricity. A report from the International Energy Agency (IEA) says that data centers used 1% of the world's energy in 2020, and this number is expected to go up. A big part of this energy use comes from software that isn't energy-efficient, which leaves a big carbon footprint.

2. **Costs of energy are going up:**
As the price of energy keeps going up around the world, software that uses less energy can help businesses save a lot of money. Businesses can cut down on their energy bills and other costs by making software use fewer resources.

3. **Pressure from regulators:**
A lot of governments and regulatory bodies are becoming aware of how the IT business affects the environment. They are putting in place stricter rules and laws that are meant to cut down on carbon emissions and energy use. Companies that follow the rules when making software can stay out of problems with the law and avoid penalties.

4. **The responsibility of businesses:**

Consumers and investors are paying more attention to how businesses treat the environment. Companies that show they care about the environment and saving energy are more likely to get investors and buyers who care about doing the right thing. Developing software that uses less energy can help a company's image and make it more competitive.

What happens to the environment when software uses too much energy?

Before getting into the rules and strategies of making software that uses less energy, it's important to know what happens to the world when software uses too much energy.

1. **More carbon dioxide emissions:**
   Software that doesn't use energy efficiently makes data centers and other computing systems use more energy. Carbon emissions go up because of this extra energy use, which makes climate change worse. Software can leave behind a big carbon footprint, and this needs to be fixed if we want to stop global warming.
2. **Running out of resources:**
   Software that isn't energy-efficient not only uses more power, but it also makes physical resources work harder. Some materials, like rare earth metals and minerals used to make gear, may be used up too quickly. The mining and processing of these materials can hurt the environment by destroying habitats and polluting waterways.
3. **Waste for electronics:**

Hardware can become useless and old too quickly if it uses old and poor software. When hardware stops working with new software, it's usually thrown away and changed. This adds to the problem of electronic trash, which can be harmful to health and the environment if it is not properly disposed of.

Tips for Making Software That Uses Less Energy

1. **Designed to be efficient:**
   To start with minimalism, remember that "less is more." Don't add features, functions, or methods to your software that aren't needed. There should be a clear goal for every line of code and every action.
   Optimized Algorithms: Pick data structures and algorithms that use the least amount of memory and processing power. Look at how hard it is to implement methods and try to make them as efficient as possible.
   Lazy Loading: Don't load and handle all the data at once; only do it when you need to. This uses less RAM and CPU.

2. **Management of resources:**

   Being aware of how your code uses energy is important for developers. Profiling tools can help you find code lines that use a lot of energy.

   Efficient Data Storage: Use storage and serialization methods for data that are efficient. When you can, compress data to save space and energy when sending and storing it.

   Memory Management: Use good memory management techniques, like trash collection and memory pooling, to lower the amount of memory you use and make your computer use less energy.

3. **Code Execution That Works Better:**

   Multithreading and Parallelism: To get the most out of your various CPU cores, use multithreading and parallel processing. But keep in mind that there may be disagreements and extra work.

   Idle State Management: Make sure that the program handles idle states nicely by using less CPU and resources. When it makes sense, put the machine to sleep or slow down the clock.

4. **User interfaces that work well:**

   Design user interfaces that look good, work well, and don't use too many resources. This is called UI optimization. Be smart about how you use hardware processing.

   User Education: Teach people how to save energy by doing things like changing the brightness of the screen or turning on power-saving modes.

5. **Testing and making profiles:**

Energy Profiling: As part of your testing method, include energy consumption profiling. Use profiling tools to find and fix code lines that use a lot of energy.

Regression Testing: Use regression tests to make sure that methods that save energy are kept up as the software changes.

Tips for Making Software Development Less Energy-Intensive

1. **Use libraries and frameworks that work well:**
   Choose tools and frameworks for software that are known for being energy-efficient. These tools are often tuned to work best and use the fewest resources possible.
2. **Take a look at energy profiles:**
   Make software with different energy profiles so users can pick between high-performance and low-power modes. For instance, a mobile app might have a "low-power mode" that lowers network and background tasks.
3. **Quick and easy data transfer:**
   Use efficient data serialization forms, like Protocol Buffers or JSON with MessagePack, to reduce the amount of data that needs to be sent over the network.
   By compressing the data being sent, you can greatly lower the amount of energy needed, especially in Internet of Things (IoT) apps.
4. **Monitoring all the time:**
   Use analytics and constant monitoring to keep track of how much energy is used and how well things are working. Application Performance Monitoring (APM) tools can help you find places where energy is being wasted.
5. **Updating and keeping up:**
   Update and manage software on a regular basis to get rid of bugs and make it work better. Software that is out of date or not designed can use a lot of power.
6. **How well cloud computing works:**
   When you use cloud services, make sure that the resources you use are optimized to meet the needs of your software. Scaling should be done automatically so that energy isn't wasted.

7. **Teach developers:**
   Teach and train writers on how to code in a way that uses less energy. Tell them to think about how their work affects the world.
8. **Hardware that uses less energy:**
   Work with hardware makers to make sure that software is made to work well with hardware features that save energy.
9. **Data centers that are good for the environment:**

Use data centers that get their power from green sources to host software. There are now many data centers that offer "green hosting" choices that can help your software leave less of a carbon footprint.

Developing software that uses less energy is no longer a nice-to-have, it's a moral and environmental must. Software that uses too much energy has effects on more than just our electricity costs; they also have effects on the health and sustainability of our planet.

It is very important for developers and businesses to use energy-efficient coding and support sustainable computers in order to lessen these effects. We can cut down on carbon pollution, protect important resources, and build a more stable digital future if we do this.

Each bit of code is important on the way to making software that uses less energy, and each developer's dedication to being environmentally friendly makes a difference. Once again, the software business needs to act like a good parent, taking care of both technology and the environment.

2.1 Code Optimization for Reduced Energy Use

Reducing the amount of energy used in software development is a very important goal in this age of global sustainability. Software that uses less energy not only cuts down on running costs but also helps make the world greener by lowering carbon emissions. This piece talks about why code optimization is important for lowering energy use, how it works, and what developers can do to make their software more environmentally friendly.

Why code optimization is important for lowering energy use

1. **Effects on the environment:**
   The amount of energy that data centers and other computing facilities use makes a big difference in carbon emissions. Code that isn't optimized makes this problem worse by needing more computer power, which means it uses more energy. By making code more efficient, we lower the amount of energy that software needs to run, which directly lowers its impact on the world.
2. **Savings on costs:**
   Companies can save money by using software that uses less energy. When you use less energy, your power bills go down, so it makes financial sense to use code optimization techniques.
3. **Commitment to sustainability:**
   As people become more aware of environmental problems, businesses are under more pressure to show they care about sustainability. Making software that uses less energy is a real way for businesses to show they care about the environment and follow the rules.
4. **Longer battery life:**

Code improvement is a key part of making batteries last longer in mobile and IoT devices. Users want their devices to last longer on a single charge, and code that works well with others is a big part of making this happen.

Guidelines for Code Optimization to Cut Down on Energy Use

1. **Make a profile and measure:**
   It's important to profile and measure how much energy the code uses before making any changes. To do this, you need to use special tools and measures to find places that use a lot of energy. The only way for developers to successfully target optimizations is to know where energy is being used.
2. **Use the CPU as little as possible:**
   The CPU is one of the main parts of a computer that uses energy.

Code optimizations should try to keep CPU usage as low as possible by getting rid of computations, loops, and busy-wait actions that aren't needed. Often, this means making programs and data structures work faster by optimizing them.

3. **Improve I/O operations:**

It can take a lot of energy to do input/output (I/O) tasks like reading and writing to files or databases. Some ways to improve I/O processes are to group requests together, use efficient data serialization formats, and cut down on file accesses that aren't needed.

4. **Dealing with memory:**

For code optimization to work, memory management must be done well. Don't let memory leak, make sure that data structures use memory efficiently, and reclaim memory whenever you can. When you use memory efficiently, you use less energy, especially on devices with limited RAM.

5. **Parallelism and concurrency:**

Concurrent and parallel processing can be used to boost speed in multi-core systems while lowering energy use. Code should be written so that it can use multiple cores efficiently without causing too much timing or contention.

6. **Management of an Idle State:**

Code should be written so that it can handle idle states well. Putting the system or gadget into lower power states when it's not doing anything is part of this. For instance, when a mobile app is working in the background, it can use less power.

7. **Algorithms that use less energy:**

Pick methods and data structures that use less energy by nature. This could mean choosing between taking more time and using more energy. Try to use methods that do as little work as possible.

Strategies that you can use to improve your code

1. **Use tools for energy profiling:**
   Use tools for energy monitoring that can measure how much energy your code is using right now. You can use tools like Intel's VTune, Linux's PowerTop, or Android's Battery Historian to find places that use a lot of energy.
2. **Choosing an algorithm:**
   Pick methods and data structures with care based on what your application needs. Choose the ones with smaller memory and computation costs, even if they take a little longer to complete.
3. **Moving code around:**
   Review and refactor code on a regular basis to get rid of duplicates, cut down on needless loops, and make logic easier to understand. When reviewing codes, energy saving should be taken into account.
4. **I/O operations that work well:**
   Reduce the number of I/O processes by using batch processing, caching data when it makes sense, and making database queries as efficient as possible. Use asynchronous I/O tasks to keep threads from getting stuck.
5. **Taking care of memory:**
   Memory profiling tools can help you find memory leaks and trends of inefficient memory use. Use methods such as object sharing and efficient data serialization.
6. **As for concurrency and parallelism,**
   For jobs that can't be done by a single CPU, use multithreading and parallelism. But be careful not to use too many threads, because moving between contexts too often can make your computer use more power.
7. **Optimization for the Idle State:**
   Put in place ways to find states of idleness and lower resource use during these times. This is very important for mobile phones and other gadgets that run on batteries.

8. **Networking that works well:**
   Reduce the amount of data that needs to be sent over the network by compressing data and using efficient methods. Cutting down on the amount of data sent over the network can save a lot of energy, especially in web and mobile apps.
9. **Testing the batteries:**
   Make sure your software works well in real life by testing it on gadgets that run on batteries. To get a good idea of how much energy you're using, use tools for battery analysis.
10. **Constantly getting better:**

Energy efficiency should be seen as a constant process. Keep an eye on and update your code on a regular basis to keep it energy-efficient, especially as the software changes.

In software creation, code optimization to use less energy is a very important task. By following the tips and ideas in this piece, developers can make a real difference in the fight against climate change while also saving money and giving users a better experience.

As the world becomes more digital, it's up to the software development group to make energy-saving methods a priority. The search for code that uses less energy not only fits with the idea of being environmentally friendly, but it also makes sure that software stays useful and competitive in a world that needs to be sustainable.

2.2 Green Algorithms and Their Application

The idea of "green algorithms" has risen to popularity in the field of computer science in recent years, reflecting the growing awareness of the need of environmental protection on a worldwide scale. The term "green algorithms" refers to computational methods and algorithms that are developed with energy efficiency and the impact on the environment in mind. This article examines the significance of green algorithms, the ideas that underlie them, and the applications that may be found for them in a variety of different fields.

The Importance of Using Eco-Friendly Algorithms

1. **Decreased Effort in Generating Carbon Dioxide:**
   By consuming less energy, green algorithms assist reduce the negative effects that computing has on the surrounding environment. This, in turn, results in lower levels of carbon emissions and makes a contribution to the effort to curb the effects of climate change.
2. **Reductions in Expenses:**
   The lower operational costs brought forth by energy-efficient algorithms make them an economically desirable option for enterprises and other organizations. A decrease in energy usage results in cheaper monthly electricity bills and an increase in the useful life of gear.
3. **Commitment to Environmental Stewardship:**
   There is a growing awareness among individuals and organizations alike regarding the impact they have on the environment. Developers and organizations can improve their public image and their sense of social responsibility by implementing environmentally friendly algorithms and thereby demonstrating their commitment to environmentally responsible computing methods.
4. **Longer Lifespan of the Battery:**

When it comes to mobile and Internet of Things devices, green algorithms are an absolute necessity for maximizing battery life. Users have the expectation that their devices will run for a longer period of time on a single charge, and algorithms that are efficient with energy play a vital part in reaching this goal.

The Fundamentals of Eco-Friendly Algorithms

1. **Analyzing the Energy Profile:**
   It is vital to profile and measure the energy consumption of an algorithm before beginning the process of building or optimizing the algorithm. Energy profiling tools assist in locating sections of

code that are particularly energy-intensive and successfully direct optimization efforts.

2. **Reduce the amount of computation:**
The reduction of superfluous calculations is a basic tenet of environmentally friendly algorithm design. In order to accomplish this, algorithms need to be optimized, the number of redundant calculations must be reduced, and efficient data structures must be utilized.

3. **Low Utilization of Available Resources:**
The goal of green algorithms is to make effective use of the system's resources. Memory management and CPU management are both included in this in order to minimize memory usage and decrease processor utilization, respectively.

4. **Parallelism and Concurrent Activity:**
Utilizing many CPU cores in an efficient manner is essential to achieving optimal energy savings. The design of environmentally friendly algorithms should focus on making the most of parallel processing while minimizing the amount of synchronization required.

5. **Optimization of the Idle State:**
It is important that algorithms be developed to deal with idle states effectively. In order to save energy, the system or device in question should shift into lower-power states whenever it is not actively carrying out any tasks.

6. **Effective Administration of Data:**

The processing and transmission of data is given careful consideration by green algorithms. It is possible to reduce energy usage by compressing data, minimizing the amount of data that is transferred, and adopting efficient serialization formats. This is especially effective in networked systems.

Implementations and Uses of Eco-Friendly Algorithms

1. **Cloud computing and data storage facilities:**
It's common knowledge that data centers use an excessive amount of electricity. The application of green algorithms to optimize data center operations, such as load balancing and server provisioning, can result in a reduction in the data center's overall consumption of energy.
2. **IoT stands for the Internet of Things.**
IoT gadgets frequently run on the limited power provided by their batteries. Green algorithms are extremely important to the process of prolonging the battery life of Internet of Things devices by lowering the amount of energy required for data processing and communication.
3. **Communication Via Wireless Means:**
Green algorithms are used in wireless communication networks like cellular networks and Wi-Fi to manage network resources efficiently, eliminate signal interference, and minimize power usage in transmitters and receivers. Examples of such networks are cellular networks and Wi-Fi.
4. **Optimizing the Use of Renewable Energy:**
In order to maximize the effectiveness of the generation and distribution of renewable energy sources like wind and solar electricity, "green algorithms" are implemented. These algorithms assist in maintaining a healthy balance between supply and demand while cutting down on waste.
5. **Transport and Logistical Considerations:**
Green algorithms are used in the transportation and logistics industries to optimize routes, reduce fuel consumption, and minimize emissions in vehicle fleets. This contributes to the development of greener transportation systems.
6. **Keeping an Eye on the Environment:**
Applications that include remote sensing and environmental monitoring frequently make use of green algorithms. They make it possible to analyse data effectively, which is necessary for

evaluating climate patterns, tracking deforestation, and monitoring the quality of air and water.

7. **Natural Language Processing (often referred to as NLP):**
In the field of natural language processing (NLP), green algorithms are a form of algorithm optimization that can be utilized for tasks such as language translation, text summarization, and sentiment analysis. They were able to reduce the amount of energy used by NLP models by lowering the computational complexity.

8. **The field of computer vision:**

The processing of images and videos in the most effective manner is the primary emphasis of green algorithms in computer vision. They are utilized in security systems, self-driving automobiles, and image analysis used in medical diagnostics.

Green algorithms are at the forefront of sustainable computing, and they offer a way toward lessening the negative impact that technology has on the environment. The adoption of energy-efficient algorithms is not just an issue of economic gain, but also a matter of moral and environmental imperative as the world continues to become more digital.

The design and implementation of environmentally friendly algorithms in software and computational systems should be given top priority by software developers and organizations. They will be able to enjoy the benefits of decreased operational expenses and increased resource use while simultaneously making a contribution to a more sustainable future if they do this.

The development of environmentally friendly computer programs requires a concerted team effort from a wide range of professionals, including not just computer scientists and engineers but also government officials, business owners, and individual customers. Together, we have the ability to harness the potential of green algorithms in order to create a digital world that is more responsible to the environment and uses less energy.

2.3 Best Practices for Sustainable Software Design

The development of environmentally friendly software has emerged as a topic of critical importance in recent years, particularly in light of the urgent need to cut down on emissions of greenhouse gases. The goal of sustainable software design is to develop applications and computer systems that, during their full lifecycles, have the smallest possible negative influence on the surrounding environment. This article examines the significance of environmentally responsible software design, provides an overview of best practices, and places an emphasis on the role that such design plays in resolving environmental concerns.

The Importance of Developing Software in a Sustainable Manner

1. **Lessening of Our Footprint on the Environment:**
   Software is ubiquitous, and a major portion of its environmental impact can be attributed to the amount of energy it uses and the amount of carbon dioxide it emits. The goal of sustainable software design is to lessen these impacts by maximizing the productive use of available resources while simultaneously improving energy efficiency.

2. **Effectiveness in Daily Operations:**
   When done correctly, sustainable software design can result in significantly more effective code and procedures. This, in turn, leads to reduced operational expenses, which include cheaper electricity bills for data centers as well as reduced wear and tear on the hardware.

3. **An Advantage in the Market Place:**
   A competitive advantage can be gained by businesses and organizations that use environmentally friendly approaches to software design. Consumers and investors are becoming increasingly lured to environmentally friendly products and services, which enhances the reputation of a business and its position in the market.

4. **Adherence to Regulatory Requirements:**
   More stringent environmental laws are being implemented by governments and regulatory agencies all over the world. The design of sustainable software helps businesses conform to these standards, which in turn lowers the likelihood of running into legal problems or being fined.
5. **Longevity and the capacity to adapt:**

The software that is considered sustainable is frequently more versatile and has a longer lifespan. It is possible for well-designed software to adapt to changing hardware and environmental standards, which can reduce the frequency with which upgrades and replacements are required.

The Most Effective Methods for the Development of Eco-Friendly Software

1. **An Analysis of the Needs and a Plan to Meet Them:**
   Considerations Regarding the Environment Be sure to include environmental considerations in the preliminary needs assessment. Take into account the software's intended usage, as well as any potential energy consumption and effects for the environment.
   Goals Regarding Sustainability It is important to the project that clear sustainability goals and indicators be established. Find out how the program can help to improve things like energy efficiency, the preservation of resources, and the reduction of carbon emissions.
2. **Architecture and design that maximizes efficiency:**
   Modular Design: An approach to design that is modular and component-based should be used. This reduces the amount of work that needs to be done to make changes that are resource-intensive and makes it possible to simplify maintenance, code reuse, and scalability.

Reduce your overhead costs as much as possible by avoiding over-engineering and over-provisioning. You should strive for a design that effectively satisfies the functional needs of the product without adding unneeded layers of complexity.

Scalability: When designing software, it is important to design it with scalability in mind so that it can adjust to fluctuating workloads without wasting resources during periods of inactivity.

3. **Coding Procedures That Are Effective:**

   Code Optimization: Compose code that is both efficient and optimized. Reduce the amount of computational complexity, get rid of any loops that aren't necessary, and use as little memory as possible.

   Resource Management: To reduce the amount of resources that are needlessly wasted, implement effective strategies for managing resources, such as allocating and freeing up memory in an efficient manner.

   Efficiency in Energy Use: Be aware of the energy impact that the code may have. Profile and monitor the amount of energy use, then optimize the sections of code that use the most energy.

4. **Effective Administration of Data:**

   Compressing Data: Both sending and storing data should involve the use of data compression techniques. This decreases the requirements for storage space as well as network bandwidth, which ultimately results in savings of energy.

   A reduction in the amount of computing overhead can be achieved by aggregating the data before processing it. This is especially helpful in Internet of Things applications that deal with huge datasets.

   Caching: In order to cut down on unnecessary data retrieval and processing, you should include caching technologies.

5. **User Interfaces That Are Effective:**

   Designing user interfaces that are both instinctive and responsive while not using an excessive amount of resources is the goal of minimalistic UI. Avoid using animations or graphical effects that aren't necessary because they use up your CPU and memory.

Screen Brightness It is important to give users the ability to modify the screen brightness, as this is a significant factor in the overall energy usage of mobile devices.

6. **Algorithms That Have Been Optimized:**

   Choose algorithms and data structures that have a lower computational complexity and use fewer resources, even if they have a somewhat higher time complexity. This is the best strategy for selecting algorithms.

   Utilize parallel processing and multithreading to get the most out of your many CPU cores, which is referred to as parallelism.

7. **Evaluation and Characterization:**

   Energy Profiling: As part of your testing procedure, include an analysis of the energy consumption profile. Utilize profiling tools in order to locate code pathways that require a lot of energy and then fix them.

   Testing for Regression: Conducting regression tests is one way to guarantee that techniques that are kind to the environment will continue to be used even when the product is improved.

8. **Deployment of Energy-Aware Technologies:**

   Choose hosting environments and data centers powered by renewable energy sources whenever it is available. This will improve the efficiency of your infrastructure.

   Virtualization: To maximize the use of available resources and cut down on overall power usage, virtualization and containerization technologies should be utilized.

9. **Education of the End-User:**

   User Guidance: Educate users about energy-efficient practices such as enabling power-saving modes, changing settings, and decreasing unneeded background operations. This is included in the user guidance.

   Transparency requires that you make it possible for people to see how much energy the software they are using consumes and how it affects their devices.

10. **Ongoing Measurement, Analysis, and Improvement:**

Tools for Monitoring Put in place continuous monitoring and analytics to keep an eye on how much energy is used and how well it is being used. Make use of monitoring technologies in order to locate areas that could be improved.

Updates on a Regular Basis: It is important to update and maintain the software on a regular basis in order to correct errors and increase its effectiveness. An excessive amount of energy might be wasted by using obsolete or inefficient software.

In a world that is becoming increasingly concerned about the sustainability of the environment, designing software that is environmentally friendly is no longer a luxury but rather a requirement. Developers and organizations are able to produce software that not only satisfies the functional requirements mentioned in this article, but also functions effectively, helps preserve resources, and has a smaller carbon footprint when they put into practice the best practices that are outlined in this article.

The move to environmentally responsible software design is a group endeavor that calls for collaboration among software developers, corporations, government officials, and end users. It is our duty to ensure that the software we use makes a positive contribution toward a more environmentally friendly and sustainable future in light of the fact that its role in our everyday lives continues to expand.

Chapter 3

Sustainable Data Centers and Infrastructure

As our world continues to become more digital and networked, there has been a sharp increase in the demand for data centers and other infrastructure that can sustain the digital ecosystem. Cloud computing, online services, streaming platforms, and Internet of Things applications are all powered by the servers and other equipment that are housed in these data centers. The fast expansion of these facilities, on the other hand, has resulted in large increases in both energy usage and environmental problems. Sustainable data centers and infrastructure have been a significant emphasis in the IT industry and beyond as a means of addressing the difficulties that have been presented.

This piece goes into the idea of environmentally friendly data centers and infrastructure, examining their significance as well as the fundamental ideas and actionable techniques underlying them. We will explore the importance of sustainability, the environmental impacts of building infrastructure that is not sustainable, and the ways in which businesses may have a positive influence by adopting environmentally responsible practices.

The Importance of Maintaining Environmentally Friendly Data Centers and Infrastructure

1. **The Impact on the Environment:**
   Data centers are notorious for their ravenous appetites for electricity, and as a result, they frequently rely on energy sources that are not renewable. Infrastructure that is not built with sustainability in mind adds to higher energy consumption, which in turn leads to increased carbon emissions and makes climate change worse.
2. **The exhaustion of resources:**
   It takes a significant quantity of resources, such as land, water, metals, and rare earth minerals, to create and run a data center. These resources are required during both phases of the project. These resources can be depleted and ecosystems can be damaged by practices that are not sustainable.
3. **Soaring Prices for Energy:**
   Infrastructure that is not sustainable can result in significant increases in operational costs for businesses as the price of energy continues to rise around the world. Implementing energy-saving strategies can assist in bringing down monthly electricity costs.
4. **Pressure from Regulatory Bodies:**
   The environmental impact of data centers and infrastructure is becoming an increasingly prominent topic of discussion among governmental and regulatory authorities. They are putting into effect more stringent restrictions and standards with the goal of lowering the amount of energy they use and the amount of carbon emissions they produce.
5. **Responsibility of the Corporation:**

The concepts of corporate social responsibility and sustainability are gaining popularity among a growing number of businesses. A company's reputation can be improved and it can better connect itself with consumers and investors who are environmentally sensitive if it implements sustainable data center operations.

The Environmental Implications of Building Infrastructure That Is Not Sustainable

1. **Unnecessary and Excessive Use of Energy:**
   Data centers that are not sustainable are energy hogs that typically consume enormous quantities of electrical power. This consumption of energy results in a rise in carbon emissions, which in turn contributes to the warming of the planet.

2. **Your Personal Carbon Footprint:**
   The amount of carbon dioxide emissions produced by data centers can be significant. since of their high energy consumption, which is often sourced from fossil fuels, data centers are a contributor to climate change since they produce a considerable amount of greenhouse gas emissions.

3. **Depletion of Natural Resources:**
   Both the building and ongoing maintenance of a data center require considerable volumes of various resources. The mining and processing of these resources can result in the destruction of habitats, the contamination of surrounding areas, and a lack of available resources.

4. **The Production of Electronic Waste:**
   Outdated computer hardware and servers can contribute to an increase in the volume of electronic garbage (also known as "e-waste") if the infrastructure is not sustainable. Elimination of electronic waste in an appropriate manner is necessary for minimizing negative effects on both the environment and human health.

5. **Utilization of Water:**

Temperature regulation in data centers frequently calls for the utilization of enormous quantities of water by the cooling systems. An unsustainable use of water can put a pressure on local water supplies, which is especially problematic in areas that have problems with water scarcity.

Principles of Environmentally Responsible and Sustainable Infrastructure for Data Centers

1. **Efficient Use of Energy:**
   A key component of environmentally responsible infrastructure is energy efficiency. This approach places an emphasis on making the most efficient use of available energy resources, cutting down on waste, and consuming the least amount of energy possible.
2. **Sources of Energy that Can Be Regenerated:**
   In order to achieve sustainability, one of the most important things to do is make the switch to renewable energy sources such as solar, wind, and hydropower. The use of renewable energy sources results in lower levels of carbon emissions and less dependency on fossil fuels.
3. **Preserving Available Resources**
   The conservation of natural resources, including land, water, and raw materials, is at the forefront of environmentally responsible infrastructure design. This includes the utilization of environmentally friendly construction materials and the effective distribution of available resources.
4. **Increased Recycling and Decreased Waste:**
   Data centers that are environmentally responsible produce as little garbage as possible and encourage recycling. This extends to the disposal of equipment, including environmentally appropriate recycling processes for electronic trash.
5. **Effective Methods of Temperature and Humidity Regulation:**
   To cut down on the amount of water used and the amount of energy required, sustainable infrastructure makes use of cutting-edge cooling methods and temperature control systems.

6. **Scalability and adaptability come in at number six.**
   A sustainable infrastructure is one that is planned to be expandable and flexible in response to shifting requirements, hence lowering the frequency with which expansions and upgrades are required.
7. **Environmental Accreditation:**

In order to demonstrate that they are making an effort to reduce their environmental impact, businesses may choose to obtain green certifications such as LEED (Leadership in Energy and Environmental Design) for their buildings or ENERGY STAR ratings for their information technology (IT) equipment.

Strategies That Can Be Put Into Practice to Make Data Centers and Infrastructure More Sustainable

1. **Optimization of Energy Use to Save Money:**
   Utilize virtualization and server consolidation to improve server utilization while also lowering overall energy consumption.
   Implement hardware with a high efficiency and use cooling technologies that are efficient in their use of energy.
   Put in place sophisticated methods of power management and monitoring in order to locate energy-wasting inefficiencies.
2. **Utilization of Alternative and Renewable Energy:**
   Make an investment in on-site generation of renewable energy, such as solar panels or wind turbines, for example.
   Get your renewable power from outside sources or from data centers that run on green energy.
3. **The Location of the Data Center:**
   Choose locations for your data centers in areas that have access to various renewable energy sources.
   Take into account the adequacy of the climate to cut down on the amount of cooling that will be required.

4. **Recovering Lost Energy:**
   Install energy recovery systems that are able to collect and repurpose the waste heat that is produced by data centers for other functions, such as the heating of surrounding buildings.

5. **Management of Available Resources**
   Utilize technologies for resource management to improve the efficiency of resource allocation and cut down on waste.
   To reduce the amount of resources needed, it is important to implement effective data storage solutions and data compression strategies.

6. **Efficient Use of Water:**
   Make an investment in water-efficient methods of cooling, including evaporative cooling or closed-loop systems, for example.
   In order to lessen your reliance on drinkable water, you should start collecting rainfall and recycling graywater.

7. **Management of the Lifecycle:**
   You can extend the life of your equipment by doing routine maintenance and upgrading it.
   Make recycling and environmentally responsible disposal of electronic trash a top priority.

8. **Green Building Design and Construction:**
   Include sustainable architectural designs in the construction of data centers, such as lighting, insulation, and building materials that have a low impact on the environment.

9. **Monitoring Efforts and Providing Reports:**
   Install monitoring devices that collect data in real time to keep track of energy consumption, carbon emissions, and resource utilization.
   Publish sustainability reports to highlight environmental accomplishments and increase transparency.

10. **Educational Opportunities for Staff:**

Provide your workers with education on environmentally responsible behaviors and urge them to develop energy-saving routines.

A more environmentally responsible digital ecosystem must have vital components such as data centers and infrastructure that are ecologically friendly. Organizations have the potential to make a tangible contribution to initiatives aimed at sustainability while enjoying economic benefits such as decreased operational costs and enhanced resource use if they adopt the principles and techniques mentioned in this article and put them into practice.

The implementation of environmentally friendly infrastructure requires a concerted effort on the part of a variety of stakeholders, including consumers, investors, policymakers, and technology businesses. It is crucial that we prioritize sustainable practices in the design of data centers and infrastructure in order to create a digital future that is more energy efficient and cognizant of its impact on the environment. This is because our digital footprint is continuing to expand.

3.1 Energy-Efficient Data Center Design

The huge variety of online services, cloud computing, and data processing that have become indispensable to our day-to-day lives are supported by data centers, which are the essential pillars of the digital age. However, the increasing rise of data centers has led to worries regarding the amount of energy they consume and the influence they have on the environment. Designing data centers to be more efficient in their use of energy has become an increasingly important strategy for addressing these concerns. In this piece, we will discuss the significance of designing data centers to be energy efficient, the essential ideas that underlie this design, as well as some practical ways for developing sustainable data centers.

The Importance of Creating Data Centers That Are Also Energy-Efficient

1. **The Impact on the Environment:**
   Data centers are infamous for their exceptionally high energy

usage, and they frequently rely on energy sources that are not sustainable. Operations in data centers that are not sustainable are a contributor to rising carbon emissions and worsening environmental degradation, which in turn exacerbates climate change.

2. **The costs of operations:**

   The amount spent on energy constitutes a sizeable component of the overall operational costs of data centers. By lowering the amount of electricity used, more energy-efficient architecture can result in significant cost savings.

3. **Preserving Available Resources**

   The acquisition of a significant amount of land, water, and raw materials is necessary for both the building and operation of data centers. Energy-efficient techniques reduce the amount of resources used and contribute to the preservation of ecosystems.

4. **Adherence to Regulatory Requirements:**

   The environmental impact that data centers have is becoming more and more widely acknowledged by governments and regulatory authorities. They are adopting stronger restrictions and standards with the goal of reducing the amount of energy that is used and the amount of carbon emissions that are produced.

5. **Responsibility of the Corporation:**

The concepts of corporate social responsibility and sustainability are gaining popularity among a growing number of businesses. A corporation that adopts a design for its data center that is more energy efficient not only lessens its impact on the environment but also improves its reputation and positions itself more favorably with environmentally sensitive customers and investors.

Design Guidelines for Data Centers That Are More Energy-Efficient

1. **Cooling and temperature regulation that are both optimized:**

   A considerable amount of a data center's overall power usage is attributable to its cooling infrastructure. An energy-efficient design will feature sophisticated cooling methods and temperature control systems to cut down on the amount of energy needed for cooling-related purposes.

2. **Virtualization of Servers and Server Consolidation:**
Through the use of virtualization technology, numerous servers can be consolidated onto a single physical machine. This results in fewer servers being actively used, which in turn minimizes the amount of energy and resources that are consumed.

3. **Integration of Renewable Energy Sources**
A important component of designing an energy-efficient data center is making the switch to renewable energy sources like solar, wind, and hydropower as soon as possible. The use of renewable energy sources results in lower levels of carbon emissions and less dependency on fossil fuels.

4. **Systems for the Recovery of Energy:**
The overall amount of wasted energy can be decreased by using energy recovery systems, which collect the waste heat that is produced by the operations of data centers and reuse it for heating surrounding buildings or for other applications.

5. **Power Distribution That Is Both Efficient and Safe:**
The utilization of efficient power distribution systems, such as hot/cold aisle confinement and high-efficiency power distribution units (PDUs), guarantees that electricity is used effectively and reduces the amount of energy that is wasted.

6. **Instruments for the Management of Resources:**
Tools for managing resources in a data center can optimize resource allocation, increasing the efficiency with which resources like central processing units (CPUs), memory, and storage are used. This reduces the amount of waste as well as the amount of energy used.

7. **A Design That Is Both Modular And Scalable:**
The design of a modular data center permits scalability, which

enables businesses to increase capacity as required without having to waste money or resources on unneeded construction or power use.

8. **Lighting that is Efficient with Energy:**
Electricity consumption for lighting in the data center can be decreased by putting in place lighting systems that are more energy-efficient. Some examples of these systems are LED lighting equipped with motion sensors.

9. **Controlling the Amount of Heat:**
Solutions for heat confinement, such as hot and cold aisle containment, are designed to separate hot air from servers and cold air supply. As a result, cooling efficiency is improved, and energy consumption is decreased.

10. **Ongoing Preventative Measures and Surveillance:**

It is vital to do ongoing maintenance and real-time monitoring of the activities of a data center in order to discover and address energy inefficiencies as well as problems in the equipment.

Strategies That Can Be Put Into Practice to Make Data Centers More Energy Efficient

1. **The Location of the Data Center:**
Choose Locations That Are Environmentally Sound It is important to locate data centers in areas that have access to renewable energy sources, appropriate climate conditions, and stable power infrastructures.

2. **Energy-Efficient Heating and Cooling Systems:**
Implementing Advanced Cooling Techniques One strategy to lessen the amount of power required for cooling is to use innovative cooling methods. Some of these methods are free cooling, economizers, and liquid cooling.

3. **The utilization of server virtualization:**
Consolidating Servers You can reduce total energy consumption

by using server virtualization to combine several servers onto a smaller number of physical machines during the server consolidation process.

4. **Integration of Renewable Energy Sources:**
   On-Site Renewable Energy: To ensure the smooth running of the data center, consider making an investment in on-site renewable energy generation equipment, such as solar panels or wind turbines.
   Purchases of Renewable Energy Make purchases of renewable energy from either external sources or data centers that are powered by green energy.

5. **Recovering Lost Energy:**
   Heat Recovery: Install heat recovery systems to collect excess heat and reuse it for heating or other purposes. Heat can be recovered for use in a variety of applications.

6. **Power Distribution That Is Both Efficient and Safe:**
   High-Efficiency PDUs: If you want to reduce the amount of energy that is wasted when electricity is being distributed, you should use power distribution units that have a high efficiency.
   Hot/Cold Aisle Containment: Install hot and cold aisle containment to separate the heated air stream from the cold air stream, which will improve the effectiveness of the cooling system.

7. **Administration of Resources:**
   Tools for Resource Allocation: Make use of resource management tools in order to maximize the allocation of CPU, memory, and storage space, hence cutting down on waste and lowering energy use.

8. **Modular Architecture:**
   Infrastructure That Can Be Scaled: When designing data centers, keep modularity in mind to maximize scalability and reduce the amount of extensive construction that is required.

9. **Lighting that is Efficient with Energy:**
   LED Lighting: Replace conventional lighting with energy-saving

LED lighting that is also equipped with motion sensors to cut down on the amount of lighting that is used when it is not essential.

10. **Keeping an Eye on Things and Doing Maintenance:**

Real-Time Monitoring Put in place real-time monitoring systems to keep an eye on things like energy consumption, temperature, and the state of the equipment.

Regular Maintenance: It is important to perform regular maintenance on all of your equipment in order to keep it operating at its optimal level of effectiveness and to replace any obsolete or inefficient gear.

The design of an energy-efficient data center is vital for minimizing the negative effects of the digital age on the natural world, while also providing benefits to companies in the form of cost reductions and improved operational efficiencies. As the digital environment continues to expand, it is essential for companies and operators of data centers to have an emphasis on sustainability and implement procedures that are efficient in their use of energy.

The shift toward the design of data centers that are more efficient in their use of energy requires a concerted effort on the part of customers, technology corporations, and policymakers. We can construct data centers that are not only technologically advanced but also ecologically responsible by adopting sustainable methods. This will contribute to a digital future that is greener and more sustainable.

3.2 Leveraging Virtualization and Cloud for Green Computing

The responsibility that falls on the technology industry to lessen its impact on the environment is only going to increase in this day and age, when environmental sustainability is of the utmost significance. The implementation of technologies that enable virtualization and cloud computing presents a potentially fruitful means of accomplishing this goal. These advancements make it possible to use hardware resources more efficiently, hence reducing energy consumption and minimizing their overall impact on the environment. In this piece, we will discuss the ideas of virtualization and cloud computing, as well as their place in environmentally friendly computing and some actionable techniques for utilizing these technologies to build a more environmentally friendly IT infrastructure.

The Importance of Environment-Friendly Computing

1. **Lessening of Our Footprint on the Environment:**
   The infrastructure of information technology, which includes data centers and servers, uses a significant amount of both energy and resources. Computing in a sustainable manner tries to reduce this impact by maximizing the effective use of available resources and energy.

2. **Effectiveness in Daily Operations:**
   The use of environmentally responsible computing methods typically results in a more effective utilization of both hardware and software resources. This, in turn, brings in a reduction in operational costs, such as lower monthly electricity bills and a longer lifespan for the gear.

3. **Measures to Reduce Carbon Emissions:**
   Computing in a way that is more environmentally friendly helps cut down on carbon emissions, which is an important step in the fight against climate change. The IT infrastructure can have a reduced carbon footprint if it uses less energy and fewer resources than it now does.

4. **Preservation of Useable Resources**
   The practice of "green computing" reduces the consumption of raw materials, lessens the amount of electronic waste produced, and prioritizes the conservation of energy, water, and other resources.

5. **Conformity to regulations and reputation:**

The importance of being environmentally responsible is being acknowledged by an increasing number of enterprises. It is possible for businesses to improve their reputation, comply with legislation, and attract consumers and investors who are environmentally sensitive if they implement "green computing" methods.

Acquiring Knowledge on Virtualization

1. **Hypervisor - see also**
   The hypervisor is the software or firmware that is in charge of creating and controlling virtual machines (VMs). It is also known as a virtual machine monitor (VMM). It allots physical resources to virtual instances, such as the computer's processing unit (CPU), memory, and storage space.

2. **Virtual Machines, often known as VMs:**
   Virtual machines (VMs) are self-contained environments for running software and operating systems on top of a physical host computer. Each virtual machine functions independently, just as if it were being run on its own specialized hardware.

3. **Sharing of Available Resources**
   The pooling of physical resources, such as a computer's central processing unit and memory, is made possible by virtualization. These resources can then be dynamically distributed among virtual machines (VMs), depending on how much demand there is. This results in improved utilization of the available resources and lower demand for the required hardware.

4. **Migrating Data and Taking Snapshots:**

Because virtual machines (VMs) can be moved between real servers without experiencing any downtime thanks to virtualization, both high availability and flexibility are ensured. Taking a snapshot of a virtual machine (VM) enables an easier backup and recovery process.

The Function of Virtualization in Environmentally Friendly Computing

Virtualization is one of the most important aspects of green computing since it helps maximize the effectiveness of resource utilization, lower overall energy consumption, and improve operational efficiency.

1. **The Consolidation of Servers:**
   Server consolidation is made possible via virtualization, in which case numerous virtual machines (VMs) can run on a single physical server. This results in fewer physical servers being utilized, which in turn minimizes the amount of power that is consumed as well as the amount of cooling that is necessary.
2. **Optimization of the Use of Resources:**
   Virtual machines have the ability to dynamically allocate and release resources according to demand. This indicates that servers that are not being utilized to their full potential can lower the amount of resources consumed, resulting in savings of energy.
3. **Increased Efficiency in the Use of Hardware:**
   Virtualization enables businesses to make optimal use of their hardware resources, thereby prolonging the useful lifespan of servers and minimizing the frequency with which they must refresh their equipment.
4. **Energy-Efficient Heating and Cooling Systems:**
   Fewer physical servers produce less heat, which results in a reduction in the amount of energy that must be used by data center cooling systems.
5. **A smaller footprint for the data center:**

Consolidating servers through the use of virtualization can result in a smaller data center's physical footprint, which in turn reduces the amount of space and resources needed.

Comprehending the Concept of Cloud Computing

1. **The Various Service Models**
   The term "Software as a Service" (SaaS) refers to one of the many

service models that can be provided by cloud computing. Other models include "Infrastructure as a Service" (IaaS) and "Platform as a Service" (PaaS). Users have access to varying degrees of control and management depending on the model they choose.

2. **Deployment Models: [Various]**
   Public, private, hybrid, and multicloud deployment strategies are all types of cloud computing environments. The model that caters to an organization's specific requirements for safety and functionality can be selected by the organization.

3. **The capacity for elasticity and scaling:**
   The resources that are available in the cloud are extremely scalable, which enables customers to supply and deprovision resources according to their specific requirements. This elasticity helps to reduce both the waste of resources and the consumption of energy.

4. **Automated systems and self-service options:**

Users are usually able to access cloud services through self-service portals, which gives them the ability to autonomously manage and expand their resources. Automation results in a further increase in efficiency and a reduction in the overhead cost of human resources.

The Importance of Cloud Computing in Relation to Environmentally

1. **Sharing of Available Resources**
   Cloud service providers share their resources among a number of different consumers and apps. Sharing resources like this results in increased resource utilization, less capacity for idle time, and decreased energy waste.

2. **Server virtualization comes in second.**
   Server virtualization is widely utilized by cloud providers in order to generate and manage virtual machines (VMs). This method

ensures that physical servers are utilized to their full potential while also reducing overall energy consumption.

3. **Data Centers That Are Efficient in Their Use of Energy:**
The most successful cloud service companies make financial investments in the construction of data centers that are designed to conserve energy. These designs may include the use of cutting-edge cooling systems, the incorporation of renewable energy sources, or both.

4. **Cooling that is Optimized:**
Cloud data centers frequently make use of innovative cooling strategies, such as free cooling and liquid cooling, in order to cut down on the amount of power required for temperature regulation.

5. **Acquiring Renewable Sources of Energy**

A significant number of cloud service providers have made public pledges to power their data centers using renewable energy sources. This results in a less carbon footprint connected with the activities of the data center.

Methodical Approaches to Making the Most of Virtualization and the Cloud for Environmentally Friendly Computing

1. **The Introduction of Virtualization:**
Server Virtualization: Consolidating physical servers can be made easier with server virtualization, which also helps cut down on power usage and maximizes use of available resources.
Desktop Virtualization: Extend virtualization to desktop environments, which enables centralized control and maximizes the use of available resources.

2. **Migration to the Cloud:**
Workloads Should Be Evaluated First: decide Which apps and Services Can Be Moved to the Cloud Workloads should be evaluated first to decide which apps and services can be moved to

the cloud.

Hybrid Cloud: One strategy to take into consideration is the hybrid cloud, which mixes on-premises infrastructure with public and private clouds to provide an optimal cost-to-benefit ratio while also optimizing resource use.

3. **Data Centers That Are Efficient in Their Use of Energy:**

   Pick Green Service Providers: Choose cloud service providers that have demonstrated a significant commitment to environmentally responsible computing and energy-efficient data center operations.

   Certifications for Environmental Stewardship Seek out cloud service providers who have earned notable environmental certifications, such as ENERGY STAR and LEED.

4. **Resource Management, Observation, and Improvement:**

   Continuous Monitoring: Set up real-time monitoring and management systems to keep an eye on how your resources are being utilized and search for areas where there may be room for improvement.

   Utilize the auto-scaling tools provided by the cloud to dynamically adjust resource allocation in response to changes in demand. This will help reduce resource wastage.

5. **Sustainable Purchasing Practices:**

   Contracts for Green Energy: If you are interested in green energy, you may want to consider purchasing cloud services from providers who get their power from renewable sources.

   Choose cloud service providers who have a priority on energy efficiency and sustainability in the architecture and operations of their data centers. This will ensure that your data is stored in an environmentally friendly manner.

6. **The Location of the Data Center:**

   Choose Your Regions Be sure to pick cloud regions and data center locations that are in line with your sustainability goals.

This should include choosing regions that are fueled by renewable energy sources.

7. **Development of Applications That Are Efficient:**

Encourage developers to build code that is both resource-conscious and efficient in order to cut down on the amount of resources that are used in a cloud environment.

Containerization: If you want to bundle and deliver programs in an effective manner, you should investigate containerization technologies such as Docker and Kubernetes.

Utilizing virtualization and cloud computing for environmentally responsible computing is not just a choice that is responsible for the environment but also a one that is strategic. It is possible for businesses to lessen their impact on the environment by adopting these technologies, which also help to cut down on resource waste and maximize resource use. The technology sector has a significant responsibility to fulfill in order to foster sustainability and contribute to the development of a more eco-friendly future as environmental issues continue to be a global concern.

3.3 Integrating Renewable Energy in Data Centers

The modern digital landscape is powered by data centers, which are crucial components that make up the landscape. Data centers power everything from cloud computing to online services and storage. Concerns about their potential influence on the environment have been raised, however, due to their ravenous consumption of electricity. A growing number of data centers are incorporating renewable energy sources into their business models in order to solve these concerns and advance the cause of sustainable development. This article examines the significance of incorporating renewable energy sources into data centers, the difficulties that are involved in doing so, as well as some practical ways for making data centers more environmentally friendly.

The Importance of Incorporating Alternative Sources of Energy

1. **Lessening of Our Footprint on the Environment:**
   Data centers are notorious for their high energy consumption, which frequently requires them to rely on sources of energy that are not renewable. Integrating renewable energy sources helps lower the carbon footprint of data centers, which in turn helps mitigate the negative impact that these facilities have on the environment.
2. **Commitment to Environmental Stewardship:**
   The principles of sustainability and environmental responsibility are being embraced by a significant number of organizations. Increasing the proportion of renewable energy used in data center operations not only complies with the aforementioned objectives but also boosts the organization's reputation.
3. **Reductions in Expenses:**
   When compared to typical fossil fuels, renewable energy sources like solar and wind power have the potential to result in cost reductions over the long run. Data centers can lessen their reliance on utility companies and stabilize their energy costs by generating their own electricity, which also helps them save money.
4. **Safety of the Energy Supply**
   Most of the time, traditional energy systems can't compete with the dependability and resiliency of renewable energy sources. This has the potential to improve the consistency and uptime of data center operations, hence lowering the likelihood of downtime caused by power interruptions.
5. **Adherence to Regulatory Requirements:**

Increases in the stringency of environmental regulations and standards are being enacted by governmental and regulatory entities. It is possible for data centers to comply with these standards and avoid penalties by switching to renewable sources of electricity.

Problems Associated with the Integration of Renewable Energy

Although it is obvious that incorporating renewable energy sources into data centers would result in positive outcomes, there are still obstacles to overcome.

1. **Intermittent occurrences:**
   Intermittent energy production can be expected from a variety of renewable sources, such as solar and wind power. They are dependent on the current weather conditions and the time of day, neither of which may coincide with the requirements of the data center's operations.
2. **The Storing of Energy:**
   Data centers require efficient energy storage systems, such as batteries, to store excess energy for usage during times of low renewable energy generation. This is necessary in order to handle the issue of intermittency, which occurs when the supply of renewable energy is intermittent.
3. **Improvements to the Infrastructure:**
   The incorporation of renewable energy sources may necessitate considerable infrastructural upgrades and adjustments to the facilities of the data center, such as the installation of new wind turbines or solar panels.
4. **Compatibility with Grids:**
   Data centers are obligated to ensure that the energy derived from renewable sources that they generate is compatible with the energy networks in their respective regions. In order to accomplish this goal, grid interconnection agreements and infrastructure investments may be necessary.
5. **The Initial Financial Commitment:**

It is possible that the installation of infrastructure for renewable energy sources would incur significant initial expenses. It is necessary for data centers to consider these expenses in light of the potential long-term advantages.

Methodical Approaches to the Integration of Renewable Energy Sources

1. **Evaluation and Investigation of the Feasibility:**
   Energy Audit: Carry out an exhaustive energy audit to gain an understanding of the amount of energy that is currently being consumed and to locate areas that could be improved.
   Study the Feasibility Determine whether or not it is possible to integrate renewable energy sources by taking into account aspects such as the location, the amount of energy needed, and the renewable resources that are accessible.
2. **Sources of Energy that Can Be Regenerated:**
   Solar Power To catch the sun's rays and turn them into usable energy, install solar panels on the roof of the data center or on ground nearby. Solar energy is widely recognized as one of the most accessible and dependable forms of renewable energy.
   Wind Energy: If there are adequate wind conditions in your area, you might want to explore installing wind turbines in order to generate wind energy. In certain areas, harnessing the force of the wind can be quite useful.
   Hydropower: Hydropower systems are capable of generating renewable energy if there is a water source available. However, they call for an exhaustive examination of the surrounding environment.
3. **Solutions for the Storage of Energy:**
   Battery Systems: Install energy storage systems that make use of batteries to store any excess energy that is generated by sources that are renewable. These batteries are able to provide electricity even at times when renewable energy generation is at a low.
   Flywheel Energy Storage: Instead of using batteries, you might want to think about using flywheel energy storage devices to provide backup power for shorter periods of time.

4. **Interconnection of the Grid:**
   Grid-Tied Systems: Establish grid interconnection agreements to sell excess renewable energy back to the grid when data centers create more power than they consume. This is possible when data centers generate more power than they require.
   Implementation of a Microgrid Create microgrids within the facility of the data center that are
   able to function independently in the event that the grid becomes unavailable.
5. **Methods for Efficient Use of Energy:**
   Hardware That Is Efficient With Energy Make investments in servers, cooling systems, and
   infrastructure that are efficient with energy to lower your overall energy demand.
   Optimize the design of the data center so that it uses as little energy as possible. This can be accomplished by effective management of airflow, confinement of hot and cold aisles, and utilization of innovative cooling methods.
6. **Surveillance and Administration:**
   Monitoring of Energy Put into place real-time energy monitoring and management systems in order to keep track of the generation, consumption, and storage of renewable energy.
   Utilizing automation to balance energy demand and supply in real time in order to maximize efficiency in energy use is the goal of automated load balancing.
7. **Acquiring Sources of Energy:**
   Purchase Renewable Energy Certificates (RECs) to offset carbon emissions connected with data center operations if direct integration of renewable energy sources is not an option.
8. **Methods That Are Efficient With Energy:**

Off-Peak Operation: Schedule jobs that require a significant amount of resources during times of the day when renewable energy generation is at its highest, such as during daylight hours for solar power.

Software Applications That Are Energy-Efficient Encourage the development and deployment of software applications that are energy-efficient in order to lessen the burden on servers.

Example: Google's Dedicated Commitment to Utilizing Renewable Energy

One noteworthy example of a company that is devoted to the incorporation of renewable energy sources into its data center operations is Google. The corporation has committed to achieving some lofty objectives, like making its data centers carbon neutral and providing continuous access to carbon-free electricity. The following is a list of some of Google's initiatives:

Acquisition of Renewable Energy Google has made investments in a wide variety of renewable energy projects all over the world, including wind farms and solar farms. These investments serve to contribute to the grid of renewable energy and contribute to the sustainable operation of Google's data centers.

Advanced Cooling Techniques: In order to lower its overall energy usage, Google uses advanced cooling techniques in its data centers in Finland. For example, the company cools the data centers with saltwater.

Efficiency in the Use of Energy Google is constantly working to improve the energy efficiency of its data centers by implementing machine learning algorithms to optimize cooling and overall operations.

Power Purchase Agreements: In order to ensure that its data centers have a consistent supply of clean energy, Google enters into power purchase agreements, often known as PPAs, with companies that generate renewable energy.

A important step in lowering the negative impact that IT operations have on the surrounding environment and moving toward a more sustainable future is the incorporation of renewable energy sources into data centers. Despite the obstacles that must be surmounted, the benefits of this initiative, which include a reduction in carbon emissions, savings in energy costs, and a dedication to acting responsibly toward the environment, make it a commendable attempt. It is anticipated that the incorporation of renewable energy sources into data centers will become an increasingly frequent practice as technological advancements continue. This will contribute to a more environmentally friendly and sustainable future.

Chapter 4

Extending Hardware Lifespan

In the lightning-fast world of technology, one of the most prevalent problems that businesses have to deal with is the rapid obsolescence of their gear. Older technology is frequently discarded before its time, which contributes to the accumulation of electronic waste and drives up expenses. Newer, faster, and more feature-rich devices and components are being introduced to the market. Nevertheless, prolonging the lifespan of hardware is not only the responsible thing to do for the environment, but it also has economic benefits. In this in-depth tutorial, we will discuss the relevance of maximizing the value of IT investments by prolonging the lifespan of hardware, as well as the obstacles that are involved and some practical techniques to optimize that value.

The Importance of Extending the Product Lifespan of Hardware

1. **Reduction in Expenses:**
   The reduction in costs is one of the benefits that can be seen almost immediately. Increasing the amount of time that hardware may be used before needing to be replaced cuts down on the amount of money that must be spent on new equipment.

2. **Methods for Lessening the Impact on the Environment:**
   The longer that companies keep their gear in use, the more they contribute to the reduction of electronic trash, also known as e-waste, and they minimize the impact that the production and disposal of electronics has on the environment.
3. **Preserving Available Resources**
   The production of hardware consumes a substantial amount of resources, including the raw materials and the energy. By extending the lifespan of gear, we can save these resources and cut down on the carbon footprint that is connected with its creation.
4. **Sustainable Development Objectives:**
   Numerous organizations have made promises and goals related to sustainability. Extending the lifespan of hardware is consistent with these objectives and displays responsible business practices.
5. **Protecting the Data:**
   When hardware reaches the end of its useful life, it is imperative that it be managed in an appropriate manner so that sensitive data can be deleted or moved safely, thereby reducing the likelihood of data breaches and compliance issues.
6. **Continuity of performance:**

Older hardware has typically been demonstrated to be more reliable because it has been subjected to more rigorous testing and has been used for longer.

Obstacles to Overcoming When Trying to Extend the Lifespan of Hardware

Extending the lifespan of hardware has a number of potential benefits, but it also presents a number of obstacles that must be overcome.

1. **The Rapid Advancement of Technology:**
   The rapid pace of technological innovation might render older hardware incompatible with more modern software and applications, hence reducing the utility of the device.

2. **Restrictions Regarding Performance:**
   Hardware that is getting on in years may not be able to satisfy the performance requirements of modern applications, which can result in decreased productivity and increased user dissatisfaction.
3. **The costs of maintenance**
   The expense of maintaining older hardware, which may include paying for repairs and the purchase of spare components, may rise with time.
4. **Problems With Compatibility:**
   When older hardware is integrated with newer components or systems, compatibility difficulties may arise. These issues need to be fixed before the integration may proceed.
5. **Dangers to Physical Security:**

Older gear may be missing important security features and upgrades, leaving it open to the possibility of being targeted by cybercriminals.

Methods That Can Be Implemented to Extend the Lifespan Of Hardware

1. **Management of the Assets:**
   Tracking Inventory Ensure that you keep an exhaustive inventory of all of your hardware assets, including details such as their age, specs, and past maintenance records.
   Lifecycle Planning: Create a detailed plan for the lifecycle of your hardware that defines the projected lifespan of each asset and the dates on which it will need to be replaced or upgraded.
2. **Preventative upkeep in the form of**
   Implementing a Preventive Maintenance program It is important to establish a regular preventive maintenance program in order to keep hardware in the best condition possible. This encompasses tasks such as cleaning, inspecting, and replacing individual components.
   Updates to the Hardware Firmware and Associated Software It

is important to ensure that the hardware firmware and associated software are kept up to date in order to address any security vulnerabilities and to ensure compatibility with newer systems.

3. **Optimizing the Work's Performance:**

   Monitoring Performance It is important to do continuous monitoring of the performance of hardware assets in order to locate bottlenecks and find places where improvements can be made.

   Allocation of Resources: Work to maximize the use of available resources so that hardware can be put to its full potential.

4. **Adjustments to Ensure Compatibility:**

   Testing for Compatibility Before updating or replacing old hardware components, compatibility testing should be performed to ensure that the new hardware will integrate without any problems with the existing systems.

   Virtualization: Run legacy programs and operating systems on more modern hardware with the help of virtualization technologies. This will allow for greater interoperability between the two sets of software and hardware.

5. **Methods of Protective Measures:**

   Erasure of Data: Before decommissioning hardware, you should use secure data erasure procedures to make certain that sensitive data is deleted completely and cannot be recovered.

   Security Enhancements: In order to alleviate the security risks associated with aging hardware, implement additional security measures such as intrusion detection systems and access controls.

6. **Upgrades to the Hardware:**

   Component Upgrades: To extend the useful life of the system, you can extend its useful life by upgrading specific hardware components. For example, you can add extra memory or replace traditional hard drives with solid-state drives (SSDs).

   The process of re-imaging involves re-installing lightweight operating systems or Linux variants that are geared for performance on outdated hardware on older computers.

7. **Efficient Use of Energy:**

   Power Management: Adjust the parameters for power management so that the amount of energy that is consumed during periods of inactivity is decreased.

   Investing in Energy-Efficient Hardware It is important to purchase equipment that is energy efficient, as this will reduce the amount of electricity it uses and the amount of heat it produces.

8. **Instruction of Users:**

   Efficient Use: Train users to maximize the efficiency and longevity of hardware by following best practices such as correct shutdown procedures and minimizing physical damage. This can be accomplished by teaching users how to maximize the effectiveness of the hardware.

9. **Support for Legacy Application Platforms:**

Application Virtualization: Make use of application virtualization technologies in order to run legacy software on more modern technology, which enables businesses and other organizations to continue using crucial programs.

4.1 Software's Role in Hardware Longevity

In the field of information technology, the connection that exists between software and hardware is one of mutual benefit. The physical infrastructure is provided by the hardware, while the software acts as the "brain" that controls how the hardware operates. When it comes to the durability of hardware, software is an extremely important factor. This article digs into the significance of software in extending the lifespan of hardware, the difficulties and factors to take into mind, as well as some practical ways for optimizing software to make the most out of IT investments.

The Importance of Software in Keeping Hardware Alive for a Longer Period of Time

1. **Productivity and the wise use of resources:**
   Software has the potential to have a considerable impact on the hardware's overall utilization efficiency. Software that has been thoroughly optimized can reduce the amount of resources that are required, hence extending the life of the underlying hardware components by lowering the amount of wear and tear they experience.
2. **Compatibility and Latest Versions:**
   Updates to your software, such as your operating system and your drivers, can improve your hardware's compatibility and fix problems. Outdated or incompatible software can put a strain on hardware, which can result in performance issues as well as a limited lifespan.
3. **Risk Assessment and Mitigation of Vulnerabilities:**
   Protecting hardware from cyberattacks requires strong software security as a prerequisite. Software that contains vulnerabilities can put the hardware at danger, which could threaten both its integrity and its longevity.
4. **Applications that Require Extensive Use of Resources:**
   It's possible for software programs, especially resource-intensive ones, to push hardware to its breaking point. Software that has been optimized can help guarantee that hardware is used efficiently, which can help prevent hardware from wearing out prematurely.
5. **Lifecycle Management, often known as**

Planning for hardware transitions in effective software management, such as upgrades and replacements, ensures a smooth transition while maximizing the use of existing hardware at the same time.

Considerations and Obstacles Faced When Utilizing Software

1. **Compatibility between Different Software**
   It can be difficult to guarantee that older technology will continue

to work with older software. The hardware might not have the necessary capability to execute the most recent software versions.

2. **Effective use of available resources**

    The use of software with a high resource requirement can put an older computer's performance and lifespan at risk. It is imperative that the usefulness of software be balanced with the constraints of available resources.

3. **Important Security Updates:**

    It can be difficult to continue to receive security upgrades for older software since software providers sometimes stop supporting legacy versions of their products.

4. **Applications from the Past:**

    Legacy apps, which may not be optimized for today's hardware, are frequently relied upon by organizations. When these apps are executed on more modern platforms, compatibility and performance problems could occur.

5. **Training for End Users:**

Users need to be instructed in the most effective ways to use software in order to guarantee that hardware is used effectively and ethically.

Methodical Approaches to Getting the Most Life Out Of Your Hardware Through Its Software

Several useful solutions can be implemented by businesses in order to overcome these issues and optimize software for the longevity of hardware.

1. **Optimisation de la logicielle:**

    Encourage software writers to build code that is both resource-conscious and efficient so that the amount of resources that are used by hardware can be reduced.

    Resource Management: To guarantee that hardware resources are utilized in the most effective manner possible, implement software resource management strategies, such as memory management and process priority.

2. **Patches and Updates to the Operating System:**
   Updates on a Regular Basis It is important to keep operating systems up to date so that you may benefit from the latest security patches, bug fixes, and performance improvements.
   Before doing an update, check to see if the newest version of the operating system is compatible with the hardware that is already installed. This will help you avoid any compatibility problems.

3. **The Virtualization and Containerization of Data:**
   Virtualization: Make use of virtualization technologies such as VMware and Hyper-V to run numerous virtual machines (VMs) on a single physical server, which allows for a more effective use of the server's hardware resources.
   Containerization: Platforms for containerization such as Docker and Kubernetes make it possible to efficiently deploy and scale applications, hence decreasing the load placed on hardware.

4. **Optimizing Applications for Use:**
   Support for Legacy apps: Invest in application modernization activities in order to upgrade or replace legacy apps with versions that are optimized for the hardware that is currently available.
   Performance Monitoring: Install tools for performance monitoring in order to detect apps that use a lot of resources and then either optimize or replace such applications as necessary.

5. **Protective Steps Taken:**
   Antivirus and Security Software It is important to ensure that your antivirus and security software is always up to date in order to protect your hardware from malware and other security threats.
   Firewalls and Intrusion Detection Systems: Protect your gear from outside dangers by utilizing firewalls and intrusion detection systems.

6. **Lifecycle Management**

    Hardware Planning: Make sure that software upgrade cycles and hardware lifecycle management are aligned in order to ensure that transitions between hardware and software go off without a hitch.

    Asset Tracking: Put in place tracking systems for your assets so that you can monitor the age and condition of your gear and plan for replacements or upgrades accordingly.

7. **Training for End Users:**

    Efficient Use: Train users to follow best practices, such as correct shutdown processes, avoiding excessive multitasking, and maintaining safe browsing habits, in order to decrease the amount of pressure placed on the hardware.

8. **Effectiveness of Energy Use**

    Power Management: Adjust the parameters for power management to limit the amount of power consumed during inactive periods, thereby extending the life of the hardware and lowering the cost of power.

    Green Computing: In order to lessen the amount of wear and tear on hardware as well as the amount of energy that is consumed, it is important to encourage "green computing" techniques.

9. **Back-ups and Continuity of Operations:**

    Backups on a frequent Basis: To safeguard against the loss of data and to ensure that hardware continues to function properly and reliably, it is important to back up data on a frequent basis.

    Creating a Plan for Disaster Recovery It is important to have a plan for disaster recovery in order to reduce the amount of damage that can be caused by unanticipated occurrences such as power outages or malfunctioning technology.

10. **Cloud and SaaS-Based Solution Providers:**

    Migration to the Cloud: If you want to offload hardware administration and benefit from the scalability and resource efficiency of cloud infrastructure, you should think about shifting to services and solutions that are hosted in the cloud.

The importance of software in ensuring a longer lifespan for hardware cannot be emphasized. When it is optimized and managed properly, software has the potential to make a major contribution to the longevity of hardware, as well as to cost savings and a decreased impact on the environment. In order for businesses to get the most out of their investments in information technology, they need to take an active role in the maintenance of their software and place an emphasis not just on effectiveness but also on security and compatibility.

The capacity to derive the greatest possible value from one's hardware holdings is a significant competitive advantage in a technical environment that is undergoing fast change. Not only can businesses improve their overall IT performance and sustainability by putting into practice the actionable solutions that are presented in this article, but they can also lengthen the useful life of the technology that they use.

4.2 Repairability and Upgradability in Software Design

The world of technology is constantly advancing, and one of the most important factors in determining the character of our digital environment is the design of software. The idea of being able to fix or improve anything is one of those fundamentals that frequently goes unrecognized despite the fact that it is of major importance. These two tenets are of the utmost importance when it comes to the development of robust and sustainable software systems, which are able to conform to shifting requirements, persevere through unforeseen obstacles, and promote expansion.

Repairability and upgradability are not simply buzzwords; they are concepts that reflect a dedication to producing software that lasts as long as possible, minimizes waste, and ensures that the digital world continues to be accessible and reliable. In this piece, we will investigate what it means to have repairability and upgradability in the context of software design, why having these capabilities is critical, and how they might be effectively implemented in a product.

Comprehending the Concept of Repairability in Software Design

When discussing the development of software, the term "repairability" refers to the simplicity with which problems, flaws, or vulnerabilities can be located, diagnosed, and remedied. It covers a wide range of facets, including as the maintainability of the software's code, the tools used for debugging, the documentation, and the general design of the product.

Maintainability of the Code The first step toward ensuring that a program can be repaired is to write code that is clear, modular, and well-structured. Having code that is simple to understand and edit makes the process of finding problems and fixing them much more straightforward. Maintainability can be considerably improved by implementing conventional coding standards, such as commenting, naming conventions, and version control.

Tools for Debugging: For efficient and prompt problem resolution, dependable debugging tools and error-handling systems are an absolute necessity. It is important for developers to have access to a wide variety of debugging tools and techniques, including as logging, profiling, and automated testing, in order to aid the rapid identification of problems.

Documentation: Anyone working on a software project should have access to thorough documentation as a critical resource. Developers are able to quickly comprehend the design and functionality of the system thanks to code that is well documented, API references, and user manuals. This aids in the detection and resolution of any problems that may arise.

Design Principles The general design of the program might also have an impact on how easily it can be repaired. Building software with a modular and decoupled architecture makes it simpler to identify and resolve issues in individual components without having an effect on the whole system. In addition, higher maintainability and repairability might result from a system that adheres to the principles of high cohesiveness and loose coupling.

Why It Is Important to Be Repairable

Repairability has an indirect but direct effect on the amount of time a software system is up and running. The quicker and more effectively problems can be resolved, the less time users have to wait while the system is offline. This is of the utmost importance for apps and services that are essential to the goal.

Software maintenance can be expensive, both in terms of the amount of time it takes and the resources that are required. The ability to repair anything cuts down on the amount of time and labor needed for continuing maintenance, which ultimately brings down the total cost of ownership.

Improving the Quality of the User Experience Users value software that operates in a dependable and smooth manner. Repairability ensures that bugs and difficulties are handled as quickly as possible, which ultimately results in a more favorable experience for the user.

Ability to Adapt to Changing Requirements: Software needs to be able to adapt when business requirements change. Software systems that are repairable are able to be modified and extended with greater ease, which allows them to accommodate shifting requirements without requiring extensive rewrites.

Comprehending the Concept of Upgradability in Software Design

When discussing the development of software, the term "upgradability" refers to the ease with which a software system can be upgraded or given new features. It has many facets, such as scalability, compatibility, and version control, among others.

Scalability refers to the ability of a software architecture to accept rising user bases and increased loads without seeing a substantial decline in performance. Scalability guarantees that the program can accommodate rising demand as well as the addition of new features without requiring significant architectural adjustments.

When upgrading software, compatibility is one of the most important considerations. Software that may be upgraded should be backwards compatible with the data formats, application programming interfaces (APIs), and user interfaces that are currently in use. The users' experience will not be disrupted, and the upgrade to new versions will go more smoothly as a result.

Management of Versions: Having an effective version control and management system is necessary in order to have upgradability. Developers are better able to communicate changes and dependencies when they use a versioning system that is well-defined, such as the semantic versioning (SemVer) system. Users are also given the ability to comprehend the implications of updates and to make decisions based on that understanding.

Why the Capability to Upgrade Is Important

Keeping Up with Technology In the lightning-fast world of technology, it is absolutely necessary to maintain your level of expertise. Software that is capable of being upgraded may take advantage of the most recent technological advances, guaranteeing that it will continue to be competitive and relevant in the future.

Updates to Security Vulnerabilities in information security are an ongoing concern. Software that is capable of receiving upgrades can have timely security updates installed, which protects user data and addresses newly discovered dangers.

Introducing New Features: Software ought to develop so that it can keep up with changing customer requirements. The capacity for upgradability makes it possible to add new features and make improvements to a system without disrupting the experience of users who are already using it.

Businesses frequently rely on legacy systems, which are unable to be quickly replaced and require ongoing maintenance and support. Software that is capable of being upgraded can lengthen the lifespan of these systems by allowing them to receive upgrades and improvements.

Repairability and upgradeability are well implemented in this design.

Consider the following: Maintainability: To get started with code maintainability, you should first cultivate a culture of it within the development team. In order to assist this effort, give developers with training and resources, and encourage developers to write code that is well-documented and clean.

Automated Testing: Make sure that any modifications made to the codebase do not result in the introduction of any new defects by investing in automated testing frameworks. Pipelines that facilitate continuous integration and continuous deployment (CI/CD) can make the testing process more efficient.

Modular Design: When developing software, it is best to adhere to the principles of modular design and create separate, interchangeable components. This makes it possible to more easily upgrade and repair individual components without having an effect on the system as a whole.

Control of Versions: Put in place solid version control systems in order to keep track of software versions and manage modifications to source code. This includes implementing a versioning system (such as SemVer) that clearly explains the nature of the changes being made.

Documentation: Give top priority to producing thorough documentation, which should include user guides, API documentation, and code comments. Check to see that the documentation is always brought up to date alongside new program releases.

Feedback from Users: It is important to actively seek feedback from users and monitor concerns that are reported by users. The input of users can be extremely helpful in determining the severity of issues and establishing priorities for upgrades and fixes.

Scalable Architecture: When creating software, it is important to think ahead to the scalability needs of the future. Take into account the possibility of rising user loads and data volumes, and build the architecture such that it can accommodate these changes.

Tests of Compatibility: Prior to launching upgrades, it is important to do exhaustive tests of compatibility to ensure that the new version will work without any disruptions with the data and integrations that are already in place.

Rollout Strategies: Create rollout strategies for the software upgrades after giving them careful consideration. It is important to think about staged rollouts, A/B testing, and rollback methods in case unforeseen problems arise.

Patching for Security Ensure that you are always aware of potential security flaws and deploy updates as soon as possible. Conduct vulnerability scans on the software on a regular basis and have a plan in place to remedy any issues that are found.

Confrontations and Compromised Options

Although repairability and upgradability are essential components of software architecture, achieving them can be difficult and requires making compromises in certain areas.

Allocation of money Spending money to maintain and upgrade software can be in direct competition with allocating resources to other development goals. Finding a happy medium is of the utmost importance.

Backward Compatibility: Backward compatibility must be maintained at all times, which can be a difficult task that can hinder the capacity to make significant architectural modifications. It is essential to give serious consideration to the trade-offs that exist between compatibility and innovation.

Building a system that is highly repairable and upgradeable can result in extra complexity if the system is not designed properly. It can be difficult to strike a balance between these principles and the pursuit of simplicity.

The costs associated with repairing and upgrading software might be significant. The benefits of having a system that is more resilient and adaptive need to be weighed against the costs of maintaining the system by organizations.

Not only are repairability and upgradability important technological considerations, but they are also fundamental design principles that must be adhered to in order to create software that can endure the test of time and adjust to the ever-changing requirements of users. A dedication to these principles can result in software systems that are more dependable, efficient, and secure, which is ultimately beneficial to both the developers and the end-users.

In this day and age, when technology permeates practically every facet of our lives, those who design and develop software have a responsibility to provide digital solutions that are not only useful in the here and now, but also environmentally friendly and flexible for the years to come. This commitment requires that our digital foundations be solid, durable, and capable of handling the challenges of a world that is always evolving. Repairability and upgradability are the cornerstones of this responsibility.

4.3 Circular Economy Approaches in Technology

The global technology industry, which is defined by its rapid innovation and ever-shortening product lifecycles, has a considerable influence on the environment. This impact can be attributed to the fact that product lifecycles are getting shorter and shorter. The linear "take, make, dispose" approach that has dominated the sector adds to the depletion of resources, the development of electronic garbage (also known as "e-waste"), and the pollution of the environment. In order to find solutions to these problems, circular economy strategies in the field of technology have gained traction. These strategies intend to move away from the linear model and toward a circular model that is more environmentally friendly and which places a higher priority on resource efficiency, product lifespan, and responsible end-of-life management. This article investigates the idea of a circular economy in the context of technology, including its fundamentals, benefits, and limitations, as well as applications in the actual world.

Recognizing the Concept of a Circular Economy in Technology

Product longevity refers to the process of designing and producing goods with an emphasis on durability, repairability, and upgradability in order to lengthen the products' useful lifespans.

Resource efficiency can be defined as the process of maximizing the use of available resources by recycling used parts, materials, and energy throughout the lifecycle of a product.

Closed-Loop Systems: The process of establishing closed-loop systems, which involve the collection, refurbishment, remanufacturing, or recycling of items and materials in order to create new products.

Eco-Design refers to the incorporation of sustainable design principles that take into account all aspects of a product's lifecycle, including its effects on the environment and society.

Product as a Service (PaaS) refers to the shift away from product ownership and toward product-as-a-service business models. In these models, customers pay for access to things rather than owning them, and this encourages manufacturers to assume responsibility for product lifecycle management.

Advantages of Taking a Circular Economy Approach in the Technology Sector

Circular technology helps conserve resources by maximizing the use of existing materials and components. This cuts down on the amount of new resources that need to be mined and processed, which in turn decreases the negative impact that is had on the environment.

Reduced Electronic Waste: Circular technology helps reduce electronic waste by encouraging repair, refurbishing, and recycling. As a result, electronic devices are kept in circulation for longer periods of time.

Cost savings can be achieved by planning for a product's ability to last for an extended period of time and by making it easier for it to be reused. This can result in potential cost savings for both manufacturers and customers.

Innovative Solutions That Prioritize Sustainability Circular design supports innovative solutions that prioritize sustainability, which in turn stimulates research and development in environmentally friendly technologies.

Resilience: A circular economy strategy in technology makes supply systems more resilient by lowering dependency on finite resources and avoiding supply chain interruptions. Circular economies aim to maximize resource utilization while simultaneously reducing waste.

Companies that embrace circular methods typically enjoy a strong brand image, which attracts environmentally concerned customers as well as investors. This results in increased profits.

The Obstacles Faced When Attempting to Put Circular Economy Ideas Into Practice Within Technology

Product Design Constraints It can be difficult to design products with lifetime and repairability in mind because of space limitations, technical constraints, and consumer desires for items that are thin and lightweight.

Behavior of customers Due to the fact that many customers are accustomed to the culture of throwaway technology, it might be tough to transition towards more environmentally friendly habits such as repair and reuse.

Chains of Supply That Are Complicated The implementation of circularity throughout global supply chains calls for coordination among a large number of stakeholders, including customers, suppliers, and manufacturers.

Changing to circular business models, such as product-as-a-service, can cause old income sources to be disrupted, which necessitates the development of new financial models.

Obstacles Caused by Regulations Existing regulations frequently favor linear patterns of consumption and may require modification in order to foster circular habits.

Applications of the Circular Economy in Technology That Have Been Seen in the Real World

Fairphone is a smartphone manufacturer based in the Netherlands that is dedicated to producing environmentally friendly and easily repairable devices. Because of the way that they are designed, consumers are able to easily repair and update components, which increases the overall lifespan of their gadgets. The ethical procurement of materials is also one of Fairphone's top priorities.

Apple's Recycling Programs Apple has introduced programs such as "Apple Trade-In" and "Apple Renew" to encourage users to recycle their old electronic gadgets by trading them in for compensation or recycling them. They have also integrated recycling robots, such as "Daisy," to deconstruct and retrieve materials from older iPhones in order to recycle them.

Initiatives for the Collection of E-waste A large number of technology businesses collaborate with various recycling organizations to appropriately collect and recycle e-waste. For instance, Dell has a free recycling program for old devices, including those that were not manufactured by Dell, in order to reduce the amount of waste that is sent to landfills.

Laptops that Have Individual Components That Can Be Replaced Or Upgraded Companies like as Framework and System76 are building modular laptops that allow users to replace or upgrade individual components such as RAM, storage, and batteries. This helps to reduce the amount of electronic waste produced and increases the lifespan of machines.

Product-as-a-Service Models: Businesses such as HP and Xerox are investigating the possibility of implementing product-as-a-service models for office machinery such as printers and photocopiers. The manufacturers are responsible for recycling, upkeep, and maintenance, while the customers pay based on how much they use the product.

Blockchain Technology Is Being Employed to Improve Supply Chain Transparency The blockchain technology is currently being utilized to improve supply chain transparency. This allows consumers to track the sources of materials and verify the sustainability claims made by businesses.

Reuse and refurbishment: Businesses such as Gazelle and Back Market specialize in restoring and reselling previously owned electronic devices. In doing so, they help cut down on e-waste and provide customers with more cost-effective options.

The implementation of methods that are based on a circular economy in the field of technology is an essential step toward achieving sustainability and environmental responsibility in the field of technology. Technology businesses can reduce their environmental impact and contribute to a more sustainable future by placing a higher priority on the durability of their products, the effectiveness of their use of resources, the use of closed-loop systems, and sustainable innovation.

However, putting circularity into practice in technology comes with its own set of issues, such as

restrictions on design, barriers posed by customer behavior, and obstacles posed by regulation. In spite of this, the move to circular technology is important because of the benefits it offers, including the conservation of resources, cost savings, and a positive image for the business.

Companies who embrace the ideas of a circular economy are likely to gain a competitive edge and help lead the way toward a more sustainable and circular future for the technology industry as customers become increasingly aware of the environmental effect of their technological choices.

Chapter 5

Sustainable Software Development Practices

A paradigm change has occurred in the field of technology as a result of the adoption of sustainable software development approaches. In addition to the more traditional goals of functionality, stability, and efficiency, the overarching objective of these techniques is to reduce the negative effects that software has on the environment and on people's ethical standards over its entire existence. It is absolutely necessary to address the environmental and ethical considerations that are involved with the development of software in light of the fact that digital technologies are becoming increasingly integrated into every area of our life.

This article examines sustainable software development techniques, focusing on their significance, guiding principles, and instances from the actual world. Software developers, companies, and society as a whole may all contribute to the creation of a digital future that is more sustainable and ethical if they follow these best practices and accept them.

Having an understanding of environmentally responsible software development

Environmental Sustainability: This dimension focuses on lowering the carbon footprint of software by optimizing resource use, reducing energy usage, and encouraging efficient coding practices. It does this by reducing energy usage, reducing energy consumption, and encouraging efficient coding practices.

Ethical Considerations Ethical sustainability places an emphasis in software design and deployment on concepts such as privacy, data security, justice, transparency, and inclusion.

Longevity and Maintainability: Sustainable software is intended to have a longer lifecycle, which decreases the amount of times it needs to be replaced or updated and helps reduce the amount of electronic trash, often known as e-waste.

Efficiency in the Use of Resources: The methods of sustainable development attempt to use resources such as code and infrastructure, as well as data storage and power consumption, as efficiently as possible.

Accessibility and Inclusivity: Sustainable software should be accessible to all users, regardless of their abilities or demographics, in order to promote inclusivity and equal access. This is necessary in order for the software to be considered "sustainable."

Open Source Software and cooperation: Adopting open-source software and encouraging cooperation among members of the developer community helps to cultivate sustainable practices by facilitating the sharing of information and code resources.

The Importance of Developing Software in a Sustainable Manner

Impact on the Environment: Greenhouse gas emissions and electronic waste are both significantly increased as a result of the growth of the technology industry. These environmental problems can be lessened with the adoption of sustainable methods.

Compliance with Regulations Companies that implement environmentally responsible business practices have a better chance of remaining in compliance with increasingly strict regulations governing the protection of personal information and the environment when they are introduced by governments and international organizations.

Long-term cost benefits for businesses can be realized through the implementation of sustainable software development practices, which frequently result in decreased levels of energy and resource consumption.

Ethical obligation In light of the growing number of issues regarding the protection of personal data, the maintenance of fairness, and the promotion of inclusiveness, ethical sustainability in software is no longer an option but rather an ethical obligation.

Reputation of the Brand: Companies that make ethics and sustainability a priority in the software development process can create a positive image for their brand, which in turn attracts customers and investors who value these principles.

The Foundational Tenets of Ethical and Responsible Software Development

Coding Techniques That Are Friendly to the Environment Efficient coding techniques, such as optimizing algorithms, cutting down on code redundancy, and eliminating activities that are resource-intensive, can greatly cut down on energy use and carbon emissions.

The practice of simplifying software design by omitting features that aren't necessary and cutting down on complexity not only helps to conserve resources but also improves the overall quality of the user experience.

Infrastructure That Is Efficient With Energy Software that is hosted on servers that are efficient with energy and the use of cloud services that utilize renewable energy sources are two ways in which the environmental effect of data centers can be considerably reduced.

Continuous Monitoring and Optimization: Constantly keeping an eye on how well software is doing and how much of its resources are being used enables proactive optimization, which in turn results in energy savings and increased resource efficiency.

Privacy by Design refers to the process of including privacy protections into the process of designing software. This helps protect user data and complies with data protection rules. Examples of privacy measures include data anonymization and encryption.

Accessibility and Inclusion as Priorities in Software Design Ensuring that All Users, Including Those with Disabilities, Can Access and Use the Software Accessibility and inclusion as priorities in software design assures that all users, including those with disabilities, can access and use the software.

Transparency and Ethical Considerations: For ethical sustainability, it is vital to be upfront about the data collecting and usage policies that are in place, as well as to take ethical implications into consideration while designing algorithms.

Longevity and Modularity: Developing software with a modular architecture and components that are simple to update can both lengthen the software's longevity and cut down on the amount of electronic trash produced.

Examples of Software Development in Real-World Contexts That Are Sustainable

Monitoring Renewable Energy Sources Sustainable software is an essential component in both monitoring and maximizing the efficiency of energy sources that come from renewable resources. Software is utilized by businesses such as Sunrun in order to effectively manage the production and distribution of solar energy.

Data Centers Efficient in Their Use of Energy Tech giants such as Google and Microsoft have made investments in data centers that are efficient in their use of energy and are fueled by renewable energy sources. These data centers make use of software that enables real-time monitoring and optimization of the amount of energy consumed.

Charging Infrastructure for Electric Vehicles Eco-friendly software is essential to the smooth operation of charging infrastructure for electric vehicles (EV). Software is utilized by businesses such as ChargePoint to manage electric vehicle charging stations, optimize charging schedules, and cut down on energy waste.

Sustainable agriculture: Agriculture technology firms such as FarmLogs employ software to assist farmers in optimizing resource utilization, reducing water and pesticide usage, and improving crop yields in a manner that is environmentally friendly.

Transportation That Is Friendly to the Environment Sustainable transportation services, such as ride-sharing and bike-sharing platforms, rely on software for efficient matching algorithms that cut down on the number of vehicles on the road, which in turn results in fewer emissions being produced.

Promoting Transparency and Ethical Sustainability with Blockchain Technology Blockchain technology is currently being utilized to assure the ethical sourcing of materials in the supply chain. This helps to promote ethical sustainability and transparency.

The Obstacles and Challenges Facing the Development of Sustainable Software

Lack of Awareness Many software developers and organizations are not completely aware of the environmental and ethical implications of their software, which leads to a lack of desire to adopt sustainable practices. This lack of awareness can be traced back to a lack of awareness among users as well.

Focus on the Short Term: Because companies typically place a higher priority on near-term profitability than on long-term sustainability, they are reluctant to invest in environmentally responsible software development.

Problems of a technological Nature: Putting sustainable practices into action might present problems of a technological nature, requiring skill in fields such as code that is efficient with energy, data protection, and accessibility.

Cost and Resource Constraints: It may be difficult for smaller firms to allot resources for sustainable software development, which frequently calls for initial investments. Costs may also be an issue.

The complexities of environmental and data protection requirements can be particularly intimidating for businesses, particularly those that operate on a worldwide scale, especially when it comes to complying with those regulations.

User Expectations Users may be resistant to modifications that favor sustainability over functionality, making it a sensitive challenge to strike a balance between user expectations for feature-rich software and sustainable development of the software itself.

The creation of a digital future that is better for the environment, more ethical, and more resilient requires the use of approaches for developing software that are sustainable. Software developers and organizations can help minimize the carbon footprint of technology, secure user privacy and data, and contribute to a digital world that is more inclusive and accessible by adopting these practices and putting them into effect.

The benefits of sustainable software development, which include cost savings, increased brand reputation, and environmental stewardship, make the effort worthwhile, despite the fact that there are hurdles and barriers to sustainable software development. Adopting these principles is not just the moral thing to do, but it is also a strategic move that will set you up for long-term success in the technology business. This is because consumers and regulatory agencies are increasingly demanding that technological solutions be sustainable and ethical.

5.1 Embracing Eco-Conscious Design Principles

The significance of environmentally conscious design concepts has never been more apparent than it is now, as the globe struggles to cope with the urgent issues posed by climate change, diminishing resource availability, and worsening environmental degradation. Design, whether it be in the realm of architecture, product creation, or digital interfaces, plays an essential part in the process of molding our surroundings and defining the behaviors that we engage in. To protect the earth for future generations, adhering to environmentally responsible design principles is not merely a choice; rather, it is a moral and ethical obligation that must be met.

This article delves deeper into the idea of environmentally conscious design, focusing on its fundamental tenets as well as the manner in which it can be implemented in a variety of different fields. We investigate the ways in which adopting these principles might lead to a world that is more sustainable and harmonious, ranging from eco-friendly product design and digital interfaces to environmentally responsible architecture.

Acquiring Knowledge of Eco-Conscious Design

An strategy that attempts to reduce the negative impact that products, structures, systems, or interfaces have on the environment while simultaneously enhancing the beneficial contributions that these things can make to society is known as eco-conscious design, sustainable design, or green design. These terms are used interchangeably. It acknowledges the interdependence of ecological, social, and economic concerns and seeks to develop solutions that are ecologically conscientious, socially just, and commercially practicable.

The Crucial Tenets of Eco-Friendly Architecture and Interior Design

Environmental responsibility: the primary goal of eco-friendly architecture is to minimize negative effects on the surrounding natural environment. This involves reducing the amount of resources used, the amount of energy consumed, and the amount of pollution produced by a product, structure, or system during its entire existence.

Utilization of Resources Efficient utilization of available resources is a crucial component of environmentally conscious design. In order to lessen the amount of waste produced and the amount of finite resources that are used up, this principle promotes the utilization of renewable resources as well as recycling and material reuse.

Sustainability: The goal of environmentally responsible design is to provide solutions that are viable into the foreseeable future. This requires taking into account the ecological, social, and economic viability of a design in addition to the effect that it will have on future generations.

Approaching a problem from every angle is essential to sustainable design, which means taking into account every stage of a product's or system's existence. This covers the procurement of raw materials, production, shipping, usage, maintenance, and either disposal or recycling at the end of the product's useful life.

User-Centered Design: User requirements and behaviors are taken into consideration during the process of eco-conscious design. The goal is to develop solutions that are not only practical but also visually beautiful and compatible with the users' beliefs and ways of life.

Biophilia: The use of biophilic design concepts entails the incorporation of natural elements, such as plants, natural lighting, and water features, into the design in order to improve one's sense of well-being and connection to nature.

Adaptability and flexibility: sustainable designs frequently have adaptability and flexibility, which enables them to accommodate alterations and adaptations as requirements shift over time, hence lowering the frequency with which they must be replaced.

Transparency and Accountability: An eco-friendly design embraces transparency in the sourcing of its materials, the procedures of its manufacturing, and the evaluations of its influence on the environment. A crucial component is having complete accountability for the supplier chain.

Examples of How Eco-Conscious Design Principles Can Be Applied

Utilizing the principles of passive solar design in the construction of a structure allows for more exposure to natural light while simultaneously reducing the amount of energy required for both heating and cooling the space.

The use of renewable and environmentally friendly building materials, such as recovered wood, recycled metal, and low-volatile organic compound (VOC) paints, helps to lessen the negative effects that construction has on the surrounding environment.

Rainwater harvesting and recycling of greywater are two methods that can be used to cut down on water usage. Rainwater can be used for irrigation, and greywater can be recycled for non-potable purposes.

The installation of energy-efficient heating, ventilation, and air conditioning (HVAC) systems, as well as smart lighting and insulation, results in a significant reduction in the amount of energy used.

Product Design that Is Kind to the Environment:

The practice of designing things with longevity in mind, allowing for repairability, upgradability, and recycling, reduces waste and extends product lifecycles. This design methodology is referred to as "circular product design."

Minimal Packaging An environmentally conscientious product designer would minimize their use of packaging by selecting eco-friendly materials and packaging solutions that are either reusable or biodegradable.

Energy-Efficient Home Appliances Energy-efficient home appliances and gadgets lower the amount of power that is consumed and reduce the emissions of greenhouse gases.

Materials That degrade Naturally and Don't Harm the Environment Biodegradable materials are materials that can naturally degrade without causing damage to the environment.

Planning and Transportation in Sustainable Urban Environments:

Public Transportation: The use of public transportation is prioritized in sustainable urban planning, with the goal of minimizing the number of individual cars on the road and the resulting congestion.

Mixed-Use Development: Cities that are planned with mixed-use projects promote walking and cut down on the need for lengthy journeys.

Building bike lanes and establishing bike-sharing programs are both examples of infrastructure that support environmentally friendly modes of transportation.

Green Spaces The incorporation of green spaces, parks, and recreational places inside urban settings leads to an improvement in both the air quality and the citizens' overall quality of life.

Designing Digital Interfaces That Are Consciously Environmental:

Coding That Is Efficient With Energy The amount of energy used by a data center can be decreased by minimizing resource-intensive processes in software and by optimizing the code for energy efficiency.

Data Centers That Are Sustainable The use of data centers that are sustainable, which are powered by renewable energy sources, helps to lower the carbon footprint of online services.

User-centered design is the practice of giving the user's experience first priority by creating interfaces that are easy to use and encourage environmentally aware behaviour. For example, energy-saving choices can be set in apps.

The Benefits That Come From Adopting Eco-Friendly Design Principles

Preserving Ecosystems and the Environment Eco-friendly architecture lessens our impact on the natural world by maximizing the use of renewable resources, decreasing our contribution to pollution, and protecting natural habitats.

Long-term cost savings can be realized for both individuals and businesses through the implementation of sustainable design practices, which frequently result in decreased resource consumption and operational expenses.

The creation of healthier and more pleasant living environments through sustainable architecture and urban planning contributes to an overall improvement in the quality of life enjoyed by those who call these places home.

Resilience: Eco-conscious design fosters flexibility and resilience in the face of environmental problems, such as extreme weather events and resource shortages. flexibility and resiliency are promoted by the use of eco-friendly materials.

Advantage in Competition: Businesses that place a priority on eco-friendly design have the potential to gain an advantage in competition by attracting customers and investors who are concerned about the environment.

Concerns and Things to Take Into Account

Initial Expenses It's possible that putting eco-friendly design concepts into practice will result in greater initial expenses. On the other hand, these expenses are frequently made up for by the savings and advantages to the environment that are realized over the long term.

Change in Behavior: Encouraging environmentally responsible habits and consumer choices can be difficult and may require education and awareness efforts.

Regulatory Obstacles The fact that already in place regulations and standards might not always be compatible with the objectives of sustainable design makes it necessary to advocate for policy changes and make an effort to comply.

The complexity of the supply chain arises from the fact that ensuring the long-term viability of all materials and components used in the production process can be difficult, particularly for companies operating on a worldwide scale.

Finding a Good Balance Finding a good balance between many design aims, such as eco-conscious design principles and aesthetics and usefulness, may be a difficult and complex challenge.

The urgent environmental and ethical problems of our time require that we address them using design concepts that are environmentally conscientious. These principles, when applied to architecture, product design, urban planning, or digital interfaces, give a road map for the creation of solutions that are responsible to the environment, equitable to society, and economically feasible. By embracing environmentally conscientious design, we can make a contribution to a world that is more sustainable and harmonious, thereby preserving the earth for both the present generation and the generations to come while simultaneously improving the overall quality of life for everyone.

5.2 Environmental Impact Assessment in Software Projects

It is necessary that the environmental impact of all human activities, particularly those connected to the development of technology and software, be taken into consideration in light of the fact that the world is facing ever-increasing environmental issues. Although software initiatives are frequently considered to be immaterial, they do leave a sizeable imprint on the environment. This is due to the energy that is used to power data centers, the production of hardware, and the electronic trash (e-waste) that is produced by devices that are used to run software. Environmental Impact Assessment (EIA) in software projects is a methodical process that assesses the effects of software development and usage on the environment.

The purpose of this evaluation is to lessen the adverse consequences and increase the likelihood of long-term sustainability.

In this article, the concept of environmental impact assessment (EIA) in software development projects, as well as its significance, essential components, benefits, and practical implementations, are investigated. Businesses have the opportunity to contribute to a more sustainable and environmentally conscious technological landscape by incorporating EIA into the software development process.

Comprehending the Role of the Environmental Impact Assessment in Software Projects

Environmental Impact Assessment (EIA) is a process that systematically assesses the potential environmental repercussions of a proposed project, plan, or program. EIA stands for the Environmental Impact Assessment Act. It helps identify, predict, and mitigate the negative effects on the environment, making it possible to carry out development operations in an environmentally responsible manner.

In the context of software development projects, EIA refers to the process of analyzing the effects that the software will have on the environment at each stage of the product's lifecycle, beginning with its planning and design phases and continuing through its deployment and eventual disposal. The major goal is to reduce the amount of damage done to the environment, to encourage sustainable practices, and to target the following key areas of impact:

Energy Consumption refers to the amount of power needed to run data centers and servers that host software programs, in addition to the amount of power that end-user devices draw from the grid.

Electronic Waste, often known as E-Waste, refers to the process of disposing of and managing electronic devices that run software. These devices include smartphones, computers, and IoT (Internet of Things) devices.

Use of materials and resources in the production and disposal of hardware components like semiconductors, printed circuit boards, and electronic components is an example of resource utilization. Resource Utilization refers to this process.

Data Center Efficiency refers to the effectiveness of data centers with regard to the amount of

energy they consume, the cooling systems they employ, and the utilization rates they achieve.

Carbon Emissions: The carbon emissions that are produced as a result of the consumption of energy and the activities of a data center.

Components of Software Development's Environmental Impact Assessments

Defining the limits of the evaluation and determining the scope of the software project are both included in the scoping process. During this stage, it will be determined which environmental consequences and elements will be taken into consideration.

Evaluation of the possible adverse effects that the software development project could have on the surrounding environment. This includes conducting research on such topics as carbon emissions, the usage of resources, and the production of electronic trash.

Analysis of Alternatives is the process of evaluating different methods or technologies that could have a smaller negative impact on the environment. During this phase, several strategies for reducing harmful effects on the environment will be investigated.

The process of developing strategies and policies to reduce or compensate for environmental problems that have been discovered is known as mitigation and management. This may involve optimizing code for energy efficiency, encouraging the recycling of hardware, or employing energy sources that are renewable.

Establishing a System for Continuous Monitoring and Reporting of Environmental Performance Establishing a system for continuous monitoring and reporting of environmental performance. The effectiveness of mitigating strategies and the continued congruence of the project with sustainability goals can be monitored by conducting regular assessments.

The Importance of Conducting Environmental Impact Assessments When Developing Software

Environmental Responsibility: Organizations have a responsibility to reduce the environmental impact of their software solutions as digital technology becomes increasingly incorporated into everyday life.

EIA helps discover opportunities to maximize resource usage and minimize waste, which contributes to the conservation of materials and energy. Resource Conservation EIA helps identify opportunities to optimize resource utilization and decrease waste.

Reducing One's Carbon Footprint In order to effectively battle climate change and lessen one's overall impact on the environment, it is vital to evaluate and take steps to reduce the carbon emissions that are linked with software projects.

Compliance with Regulations Numerous countries and areas have enacted environmental regulations and standards, which compel businesses to evaluate the negative effects of their actions on the environment and take steps to lessen or eliminate those effects.

EIA is in line with the principles of sustainable development, which helps to ensure that software projects make a beneficial contribution to achieving environmental, social, and economic goals.

Advantages to Be Obtained by Conducting Environmental Impact Assessments on Software Projects

The Environmental Impact Assessment (EIA) helps maintain ecosystems, conserve resources, and lower pollution levels by analyzing potential adverse effects on the environment and developing strategies to mitigate those effects.

Savings on Costs: Optimising the use of resources and reducing energy consumption can frequently result in cost savings for businesses, both in terms of their monthly energy costs and their resource acquisition.

Compliance with Regulations: EIA helps to guarantee that software projects are in line with environmental regulations, hence lowering the possibility of incurring both monetary and legal fines.

Improved Reputation: Businesses that place a high priority on their environmental responsibilities enjoy an improved reputation, which helps them recruit consumers, partners, and investors that are environmentally conscientious.

Innovation and Efficiency: The EIA promotes innovation in software design and development, which helps to pave the way for the development of technologies that are more energy-efficient and environmentally friendly.

Applications of Environmental Impact Assessment in Software Development from a Practical Standpoint

Programming Techniques That Save Energy Developers can adopt programming techniques that save energy by optimizing algorithms, limiting resource-intensive processes, and eliminating idle processing.

Efficiency of Data Centers: Corporations are able to evaluate and enhance the energy efficiency of their data centers by maximizing server utilization, utilizing energy-efficient hardware, and deploying advanced cooling systems. These three practices are collectively referred to as "data center efficiency."

Sources of Renewable Energy: Software hosting can have a substantially smaller carbon footprint if it is fueled by renewable energy sources such as wind, solar, or hydroelectric power, which data centers can get their power from.

End-of-Life Management: Organizations can encourage responsible end-of-life management of electronic devices by promoting recycling, refurbishing, or donation programs for outdated hardware. This is one way to promote responsible end-of-life management of electronic devices.

Offsetting Carbon Emissions: Organizations can invest in carbon offset programs or renewable energy projects in order to offset the carbon emissions that are linked with software development initiatives.

Concerns and Things to Take Into Account

Obtaining Reliable statistics It may be difficult to acquire reliable statistics on energy usage, resource utilization, and carbon emissions, particularly for cloud-based services and hosting provided by third parties.

Behavior Modification: Encouraging eco-conscious habits among software developers and end-users can be a big issue that requires education and awareness. In order to be successful, this change in behavior is essential.

Considerations Regarding expenditures Despite the fact that EIA might result in cost reductions over the long term, some firms may be hesitant to invest in sustainability measures due to the initial expenditures involved.

Maintaining a Healthy Balance It can be difficult to maintain a healthy balance between eco-conscious design principles and other project goals, such as functionality, performance, and the user experience.

An Environmental Impact Assessment (EIA) for software projects is an essential action to take in order to create a technological landscape that is more sustainable and environmentally conscientious. Organizations are able to minimize the amount of damage done to the environment, lower the amount of resources they use, and contribute to a future that is more sustainable if they carefully evaluate the environmental impact of the development and use of software. Integration of environmental impact assessments (EIA) into software development projects is no longer an option but an ethical and environmental need for responsible and eco-conscious technological innovation. This is because the relevance of environmental concerns is continuing to grow.

5.3 Cultivating a Culture of Sustainability

The importance of maintaining a sustainable environment is becoming more and more obvious in the modern society. The growing worldwide concerns of climate change, resource depletion, and environmental degradation highlight the necessity for firms to embrace sustainability not simply as a trend but as a fundamental component of their corporate culture. The cultivation of a culture of sustainability needs a profound transformation in thinking and values, where environmental responsibility becomes ingrained in the very fabric of a company. This goes much beyond the implementation of merely cosmetic green projects.

In this piece, we go into the idea of a culture of sustainability, discussing its significance, important components, and critical tactics for encouraging environmental responsibility inside enterprises. Adopting a culture of sustainability can lead to beneficial environmental and social consequences, while also improving the long-term resilience and reputation of an organization. This is true whether the organization in question is a for-profit business, a nonprofit organization, a government agency, or an educational institution.

Acquiring an Understanding of Sustainability Culture

The collective beliefs, values, behaviors, and practices of a company that place an emphasis on environmental stewardship, social responsibility, and economic viability are all components of what is known as a culture of sustainability. It entails incorporating principles of sustainable development into each and every area of an organization's activities, decision-making processes, and interactions with stakeholders.

The Crucial Components That Make Up a Culture of Sustainability

Recognition of an Organization's obligation to reduce Its Negative Impact on the Environment is Essential to a Culture of Sustainability

The recognition of an organization's obligation to reduce its negative impact on the environment is essential to a culture of sustainability. This includes lowering the amount of resources that are used, cutting down on waste, and cutting down on carbon emissions.

In addition to worries about the natural environment, sustainability also takes into account issues of social fairness and encourages inclusiveness. It is imperative that businesses work hard to cultivate a culture in the workplace that values diversity, equity, and inclusion on both the company's internal and external fronts.

Economic survival Rather than being viewed as a financial burden, a culture of sustainability should be viewed as a tool to ensure the organization's long-term economic survival. The adoption of sustainable practices may result in financial savings, improvements in operational efficacy, and new business possibilities.

Engagement of Stakeholders: It is essential for a business to engage with its various stakeholders, such as its employees, customers, and suppliers, as well as the community in which it operates. It is imperative that organizations address their issues and take their input into consideration during the decision-making process.

Accountability and Transparency: Two of the most important aspects of a sustainable culture are the accountability for achieving sustainability objectives and the disclosure of information regarding sustainability activities. It is important for organizations to be transparent about their activities, including their triumphs and difficulties.

Learning Without Stopping and Always Striving to Do Better Both of these are highly valued in a culture that promotes sustainability. It is important for organizations to be receptive to input, flexible in the face of shifting conditions, and persistent in their pursuit of methods to improve their sustainability performance.

The Significance of Incorporating a Culture of Sustainability

Stewardship of the Environment: A sustainable culture assists organizations in lowering their environmental footprint, which in turn helps to mitigate the effects of climate change, preserve ecosystems, and conserve resources.

Organizations that place a priority on sustainability contribute to social equity through promoting diverse and inclusive workplaces, providing assistance to local communities, and preserving ethical business practices.

Economic Resilience: An organization's long-term economic resilience can be increased by implementing sustainable practices because these activities frequently result in cost reductions, improved operational efficiency, and innovation.

A culture of sustainability may attract and keep individuals who are enthusiastic about environmental and social responsibility, which can lead to a workforce that is more motivated and engaged in its job.

Enhanced Reputation: Businesses that demonstrate a commitment to sustainability typically have a positive reputation, which helps attract consumers, partners, and investors that are environmentally sensitive.

Methods for the Promotion of a Culture of Environmental Stewardship

Commitment from Leadership: Leadership is one of the most important factors in determining the tone that will be established for a culture that values sustainability. The most effective leaders are those who can express a crystal-clear vision, set attainable goals related to sustainability, and lead by example.

Integration into Strategy: It is important for a company to incorporate sustainability into both the strategic planning and decision-making processes of the organization. As a result, this ensures that issues of sustainability are placed at the forefront of all actions.

Education and Training: Providing staff at all levels with education and training on the concepts and practices of sustainability is an effective way to raise awareness and create the essential skills.

Establishing Cross-Functional Teams It is important to establish cross-functional sustainability teams that will bring together professionals from a variety of departments in order to design and put into action sustainability ideas in a cooperative manner.

Setting Measurable Goals: Defining specific, measurable, achievable, relevant, and time-bound (SMART) sustainability goals enables businesses to track progress and hold themselves responsible. SMART stands for "specific, measurable, achievable, relevant, and time-bound."

Participation of Stakeholders: Participation of stakeholders, such as employees, consumers, suppliers, and communities, is essential to the achievement of sustainable development. Make an effort to get their comments and incorporate it into the sustainability projects you're developing.

Sustainable Procurement Selecting suppliers and partners that share your commitment to maintaining high ethical and environmental standards is an important step in the implementation of sustainable procurement policies.

Reporting on Sustainability Publish sustainability reports on a regular basis that communicate in

an open and honest manner your organization's progress and the problems it has in attaining its sustainability goals.

Fostering a culture of appreciation for sustainable initiatives can be accomplished through the use of recognition and rewards. Individuals and teams who display an exceptional dedication to sustainability should be recognized and rewarded.

Continuous Improvement: A road toward sustainability is something that never ends. Evaluating and re-evaluating sustainability programs, adjusting to ever-shifting conditions, and looking for fresh chances for improvement should be ongoing activities.

Organizations That Have Strong Cultures of Sustainability That Serve as Examples

Patagonia: The outdoor clothing manufacturer Patagonia is well-known for its unwavering dedication to environmental protection and preservation. They encourage customers to repair and reuse their items and place a priority on being environmentally responsible. They also source their materials in an ethical manner.

Unilever, a global leader in consumer goods, has made a commitment to making sustainability an integral component of its overall business strategy. They have set lofty sustainability targets for themselves, such as recycling, composting, or reusing all of their plastic packaging by the year 2025.

Google: Google has already achieved carbon neutrality and has made a commitment to run solely on renewable energy in the future. Additionally, the corporation makes financial contributions to programs relating to renewable energy and invests in research on sustainable practices.

IKEA: The Swedish home furnishings firm IKEA has set a goal to become climate neutral by the year 2030. In order to cut down on waste, they give precedence to environmentally friendly materials, products that are efficient with energy, and circular design principles.

Flooring manufacturer Interface is committed to environmentally responsible business practices and the concept of a circular economy. They have pledged to eradicating any negative influence on the environment by the year 2040 and are well-known for the transparency of their reports regarding sustainability.

Concerns and Things to Take Into Account

Resistance to Change There is a possibility that some employees will oppose sustainability initiatives out of fear of being disrupted or a lack of knowledge.

Constraints Placed on Resources The implementation of sustainability projects can call for initial investments in terms of both time and money, as well as human resources.

Initiatives aimed at achieving sustainability might be difficult due to the involvement of a wide variety of departments, stakeholders, and factors.

Impact Evaluation: Evaluating the results of sustainability initiatives can be difficult and calls for the creation of suitable metrics and data collection mechanisms.

Organizations may have difficulty striking a balance between their sustainability aims and other conflicting priorities, such as increasing profitability and expanding their customer base.

The development of a culture that is sustainable is not merely a worthy goal; rather, it is an essential commitment that must be made in order to achieve environmental responsibility, social equity, and economic viability. We may make a contribution to a world that is more sustainable and harmonious if we incorporate sustainability ideas into the fundamental beliefs and practices of the companies we work for. Adopting a culture of sustainability is not just a moral and ethical obligation, but also a strategic choice that strengthens organizational resilience and reputation in an ever-evolving global landscape. This is true regardless of whether one works in business, government, nonprofits, or academic institutions.

Chapter 6

Challenges and Future Trends

The fast-paced and linked world we live in today is home to ever-evolving problems and future trends, which in turn shape the way we live, work, and interact with one another. This article goes into some of the most important problems that society is currently facing and investigates some of the rising trends that are anticipated to define the future. This in-depth research intends to throw light on the complex terrain of challenges and opportunities in the 21st century, ranging from technical developments to environmental issues, social transformations, and economic shifts. The goal of this analysis is to shed light on these complicated landscapes.

1. **Technological Difficulties and Prospective Developments: Dangers posed by Cyberspace:**
   Individuals, companies, and even governments are increasingly susceptible to cyberattacks
   because of their growing reliance on digital technologies. To keep one step ahead of hackers, the trend going forward will be to develop more sophisticated cybersecurity solutions that include the

incorporation of artificial intelligence (AI) and machine learning.

Automation and the use of artificial intelligence:
The proliferation of artificial intelligence and automation is causing industries to undergo profound changes, which has raised concerns about the loss of jobs as well as ethical questions. The difficulty lies in figuring out how to put these technologies to use for the benefit of society while simultaneously minimizing any potential adverse effects.

Inclusion in the Digital Age:
The digital divide, which refers to the gap between those who have access to digital tools and those who do not, is widening as technology continues to improve. This chasm will likely be closed in the near future by means of programs and efforts that guarantee equal access to technological resources and instruction in digital literacy.

Privacy and the Moral Treatment of Data:
The gathering and use of personal information raises ethical problems regarding privacy and permission. There is a good chance that future developments will include more stringent data restrictions, an increase in openness, and the development of decentralized data management technologies such as blockchain.

2. **Environmental Difficulties and Prospective Developments:**
The Influence of Climate:
The issue of climate change is still one of the most important concerns facing the world today. In the not too distant future, we will see a shift toward the use of renewable energy sources, environmentally responsible agricultural practices, and increased international collaboration aimed at lowering emissions of greenhouse gases.

Loss of Biological Diversity:
Both the health of ecosystems and people are put in jeopardy by the fast loss of biodiversity. The practice of sustainable land management, reforestation, and conservation are all emerging as

important future themes.
Limited Access to Resources:
Future generations are going to face difficulties as a result of the depletion of natural resources such as freshwater and minerals. Recycling of resources, the creation of alternative materials, and the development of models for circular economies are all current trends.

3. **Social Difficulties and Prospective Developments:**
Changes in the Demographic Makeup:
In many countries, social systems and economic progress are being challenged by populations that are getting older while birth rates are falling. Immigration as a means of redressing demographic inequalities and policies designed to support an aging workforce are two examples of emerging trends.
Wellness of the mind:
Problems with mental health are on the rise, and factors such as social isolation and stress are contributing to this trend. In the not-too-distant future, we will see an increase in awareness and destigmatization of mental health issues, as well as the incorporation of mental health support services into existing healthcare systems.
Inequality in Society :
Continued significant societal obstacles include, but are not limited to, economic inequities, racial inequalities, and access to education. Experiments with universal basic income and education reforms are two examples of potential future trends that entail strategies to lessen inequality.

4. **Economic Difficulties and Prospective Developments:**
Uncertainty Regarding the Global Economy:
The need for economic resilience has been more apparent in recent years as a result of factors including economic volatility, trade tensions, and the impact of unanticipated events such as the COVID-19 pandemic. The future will likely see a greater

emphasis placed on international cooperation and the diversification of supply chains.

The Impact of Mechanization on Employment:
The steadily growing rate at which employment are being automated presents difficulties for the labor force. Programs for reskilling and upskilling workers are expected to become increasingly popular in the coming years, as will the creation of new job opportunities in developing sectors.

Growth in the Economy That Is Stable:
A primary objective should be to achieve sustainable economic growth that strikes a healthy balance between economic prosperity, environmental health, and social well-being. The implementation of sustainable business practices and the principles of the circular economy will be prominent in future trends.

5. **Political Difficulties and the Direction of the Future:**

Tensions in International Politics:
Rivalries and wars in geopolitics pose a threat to the stability of the global environment. Diplomacy, multilateral collaboration, and efforts to resolve conflicts are going to be increasingly important in the future.

The Weakening of Democracy:
Concerns have been raised regarding the future of governance as a result of the weakening of democratic institutions in various countries. The promotion of transparency, the strengthening of democratic institutions, and the defense of human rights are all tendencies that are likely to emerge in the future.

Protection of the World's Health:
The COVID-19 epidemic brought to light weaknesses in the health care systems of multiple countries. In the years to come, we will see an increase in the level of readiness for pandemics, investments in healthcare infrastructure, and the fortification of international health organizations.

In our world that is continuously changing, the challenges and opportunities that lie ahead are varied and interwoven. In order to overcome these obstacles, a concerted effort on the part of multiple governments, businesses, and social groups is required. Despite the fact that the problems are enormous, the trends of the future provide hope as well as opportunity for constructive change. In order to construct a future that is more sustainable and equitable for all people, it is necessary to take important initiatives such as embracing technological breakthroughs, reducing environmental hazards, fostering social inclusion, assuring economic resilience, and promoting political stability. We are able to handle the intricacies of our ever-changing world and make strides toward a better tomorrow if we acknowledge these obstacles and take action in response to them.

6.1 Overcoming Barriers to Green Computing Adoption

In today's technology-driven society, the concept of "green computing," which is also known as "sustainable computing" or "eco-friendly computing," is an essential one. Its primary goals are to lessen the damage that computing systems cause to the natural world and to encourage the adoption of environmentally responsible business practices within the information technology sector. Even while it is clear that green computing has many advantages, there are still several obstacles in the way of its widespread adoption. The need of making the switch to computing habits that are less harmful to the environment is emphasized throughout this article, which investigates various roadblocks and provides strategies for overcoming them.

1. **Comprehending the Meaning of "Green Computing"**
   Energy efficiency refers to the process of lowering overall energy usage in buildings such as businesses, houses, and data centers by optimizing the design of hardware and software.
   Management of e-waste refers to the act of correctly disposing of and recycling electronic trash in order to reduce the amount of harmful substances that are discharged into the environment.

Conserving resources involves reducing resource consumption as much as possible by maximizing the usage of virtualization and cloud computing and extending the lifespan of physical hardware.

Choosing environmentally friendly components and materials during the buying process is an example of sustainable procurement.

2. **Obstacles to the Implementation of Green Computing:**

Concerns About the Price:

The misconception that environmentally responsible computing activities come at a high cost is one of the most significant obstacles. It is possible for enterprises to incur early expenditures that they are hesitant to pay, such as those associated with educating personnel, upgrading data centers, and investing in energy-efficient gear.

Insufficient Knowledge, Awareness, and Education:

A significant number of people and organizations do not have a complete understanding of the effects that their computer behaviors have on the surrounding environment. This ignorance contributes to a resistance to change, which in turn hinders progress.

Opposition to the Process of Change:

As a general rule, humans are averse to change, and as a result, some people may be reluctant to adopt new environmentally friendly computing practices or technology.

Obstacles Presented by Regulators:

There may be a lack of rules that are consistent across regions or that are particularly rigorous regulating the disposal of electronic trash and the use of energy. This can function as a disincentive for businesses to embrace environmentally friendly computing methods.

Systems Left Behind:

Many companies are still using antiquated technology that isn't friendly to the environment or sustainable. It may be difficult to replace or upgrade these systems due to compatibility concerns as well as the accompanying expenses.

Concentration on the Near-Term

Some corporations place a higher value on short-term financial profits than they do on the long-term benefits to the environment. It's possible that they don't see the point in investing in environmentally friendly computing solutions.

3. **Methods for Overcoming Obstacles:**

Solutions That Are More Economical:

It is important to encourage the creation and acceptance of environmentally friendly computer technologies that are also cost effective. In the long run, investing in energy-efficient hardware and engaging in sustainable activities typically results in cost savings. This is accomplished through decreased energy bills and an increased lifespan for the equipment.

The importance of education and awareness:

To educate individuals and organizations about the environmental impact of their computer activities, awareness campaigns and training programs should be launched and provided, respectively. Put more emphasis on the long-term advantages of eco-friendly computing.

Encouragements in the Form of Tax Breaks:

Organizations that embrace environmentally responsible computing methods may be eligible for financial incentives, tax rebates, or grants from governing bodies and regulatory agencies. This may assist offset some of the costs associated with the first investment.

Frameworks for Regulatory Compliance:

Regulate the disposal of electronic waste, improve energy efficiency, and promote sustainable purchasing practices, and ensure that these policies are consistent and environmentally beneficial. These restrictions have the potential to provide enterprises with a level playing field.

Upgrades for Legacy Systems :
Provide companies with the financial help or incentives they need to upgrade or replace their outdated systems with alternatives that are more energy efficient. Place an emphasis on the long-term benefits and return on investment that such enhancements can provide.

Showcase Some Examples of Your Achievements:
Bring to light case studies and success stories involving businesses that have effectively adopted environmentally responsible computing practices. This might act as both an example and a validation of the concept for other people.

Working Together and Forming Partnerships:
Encourage collaboration between national governments, environmental organizations, and the leaders of various industries. These alliances have the potential to accelerate research, development, and implementation of environmentally friendly computing technologies.

4. **Best Practices for Environmentally Friendly Computing:**

Hardware that Is Effective in Saving Energy:
Make an investment in computers, servers, and data centers that are efficient in their use of energy. In order to cut down on energy consumption, it is important to look for items that have been awarded the ENERGY STAR certification and to explore virtualization and cloud computing.

Controlling the Power:
Turn on the energy-saving features of your computer and any other devices you use. Put in place procedures that will automatically shut down systems when they are idle.

Energy from renewable sources:
It is a good idea to get the power needed for your offices and data centers from renewable resources such as the wind or the sun.

Recycling of Electronic Waste:

Create recycling programs for electronic waste to ensure the environmentally appropriate
disposal of outdated hardware. To the extent that it is feasible, you should encourage the repair and refurbishment of electronic gadgets.

Sustainable Purchasing Practices:

During the purchasing process, give preference to products and materials that are less harmful to the environment. Take into account every stage of the product's life, from its creation to its eventual disposal.

Telecommuting and other forms of remote work:

Adopting regulations that allow for workers to do their duties away from the traditional office setting can cut down on the amount of time spent commuting as well as the amount of energy required to run the business.

Environment-Friendly Data Centers:

Put into practice methods of data center cooling and power delivery that offer the highest possible level of energy efficiency. Utilize tactics that are effective for server consolidation and virtualization.

Keeping an Eye on Things and Filing Reports:

Maintain consistent monitoring and reporting of energy consumption as well as the impact on the environment. Further progress can be made through increased transparency.

In today's fast evolving world, the implementation of environmentally responsible computing methods is not only a morally sound decision but also a practical one. A concerted effort from individuals, organizations, governments, and the technology industry is required to overcome the challenges that prevent the widespread adoption of environmentally friendly computing. We can pave the path for a more sustainable and environmentally friendly future in computing by resolving concerns about cost, creating awareness, implementing regulatory frameworks, and displaying success stories in the industry. In addition, adopting the best practices in green computing is crucial to lowering the environmental effect of IT operations and maintaining a healthy planet for future generations. This can be accomplished by minimizing the amount of energy used by computers.

6.2 Emerging Technologies and Future Prospects

A technological revolution is currently taking place all across the planet. The rate at which existing and emerging technologies are altering businesses, economies, and communities is unparalleled. These technologies have the potential to bring about significant changes in the way we live our lives, the way we work, and the way we interact with one another. In this piece, we will examine a number of important new technologies and their potential applications in the future, putting light on the opportunities and difficulties that these technologies provide.

1. **Synergy between Artificial Intelligence (AI) and Machine Learning:**

   Autonomous Systems: Artificial intelligence (AI) that powers autonomous cars, drones, and robots is on the cusp of ushering in a new era of innovation in the transportation, logistics, and manufacturing industries.

   The healthcare industry anticipates that the application of AI will improve diagnostics, medication discovery, and personalized therapy, ultimately leading to better patient outcomes and lower overall costs.

   The application of machine learning algorithms in the financial services industry for activities such as fraud detection, risk assessment, and algorithmic trading has the potential to reshape the business.

   Natural Language Processing: Advances in language comprehension and generation will make it possible to create more advanced chatbots, as well as improvements in language translation and original content creation.

   Ethical and Regulatory Challenges: It will be essential for responsible AI deployment to address ethical concerns associated to AI, such as bias and privacy.

2. **Computing on the Quantum Level:**
   Complex Problem Solving It is possible that quantum computers may be able to tackle difficult problems such as optimization, cryptography, and material simulations far more quickly than classical computers will be able to.
   Simulation of molecular interactions, which is made possible by quantum computing, can speed up the process of drug discovery, which in turn can lead to the development of new medications and therapies.
   Scalability Issues Constructing quantum computers that are both useful and large-scale is a big technical difficulty, however there has been some forward movement in this area.
   Cybersecurity: Quantum computing, despite the fact that it has the ability to break currently used encryption systems, also presents the possibility of developing quantum-safe cryptography.
3. **The Internet of Things (IoT)**
   Smart Cities The Internet of Things provides more effective resource management, traffic control, and urban planning, all of which contribute to the growth of smart cities.
   In the field of medicine, Internet of Things devices can be used to perform remote patient monitoring, advance medical diagnosis, and improve the quality of healthcare delivery.
   Agriculture: Optimizing farming methods through the use of IoT sensors and data analytics can lead to improved crop yields and more environmentally friendly agriculture.
   Privacy and Safety Ensuring the confidentiality and safety of data collected by IoT devices is still an extremely difficult task.
4. **Technology Based on 5G:**

Enhanced Mobile Connectivity: 5G will allow for faster downloads, increased streaming quality, and enhanced opportunities for mobile gaming.

Acceleration of Internet of Things: The low latency and high bandwidth of 5G make it perfect for linking Internet of Things devices, hence paving the door for more widespread use of IoT.

Edge Computing: 5G networks will make edge computing easier, which is a form of data processing in which data is processed closer to its source. This helps reduce latency for applications that are time-sensitive.

modifications to the Infrastructure The deployment of 5G networks calls for considerable modifications to the infrastructure, including the construction of tiny cells and fiber-optic connections, among other things.

Biotechnology and genetic engineering are next on the agenda

Precision medicine refers to the practice of tailoring medical treatments to an individual based on that person's genetic make-up. This could result in more effective and individualized medical care.

Gene Editing Using CRISPR: The CRISPR-Cas9 technique for editing genes offers the potential to treat genetic illnesses and generate genetically modified organisms with the qualities that are wanted.

Agricultural Innovation: The use of genetic engineering can increase crop yields, improve crop resilience, and decrease the amount of pesticides that are required.

Ethical and Regulatory Considerations It is necessary to strike a balance between the advancement of science and ethical considerations as well as regulatory frameworks.

VI. Methods of Energy Regeneration and Environmentally Friendly Technology:

Solar Energy: Recent developments in solar panel technology are making solar energy a more viable option both in terms of efficiency and cost.

Energy Storage: Advances in battery technology are essential for the storage and distribution of renewable energy sources like solar and wind power.

Vehicles Powered by Electricity It is anticipated that the widespread adoption of electric vehicles (EVs) will lead to a reduction in the emissions of greenhouse gases caused by transportation.

Economy Revolving Around Itself The use of sustainable materials and recycling procedures can both reduce waste and promote an economy that revolves around itself.

AR and VR stand for augmented reality and virtual reality, respectively.

Learning That Is Completely Immersive Augmented and virtual reality have the potential to transform education by producing learning environments that are wholly immersive.

Virtual tourism is made possible by virtual reality (VR), which enables users to experience travel to new locations without physically leaving their homes.

Training and Simulation: Aviation, healthcare, and the military are some of the businesses that use augmented reality and virtual reality for training purposes.

Hardware Improvements The continued development of augmented reality (AR) and virtual reality (VR) headsets will make these technologies more approachable and immersive in the near future.

The Technology Behind the Blockchain:

Blockchain technology has the potential to improve supply chain management by increasing transparency and traceability, hence lowering the risk of fraud and errors.

The use of intermediaries can be minimized through the use of smart contracts, which are computer programs that can automatically carry out the terms of a contract.

Improved Authentication and Privacy thanks to Blockchain Technology Blockchain technology can give digital identities that are both secure and verified.

Regulatory Obstacles: It will be difficult to solve the regulatory and legal problems that are associated with blockchain technology.

IX. Aerospace Innovations and the Exploration of Outer Space:

Mars colonization: There are now ongoing efforts being made by space agencies as well as commercial firms to construct human settlements on Mars.

Space Tourism: The development of space tourism has the potential to make space travel available to the general public.

Satellite Technology: Developments in satellite technology are leading to improvements in communication, as well as in navigation and the ability to observe Earth.

Challenges of crucial importance include ensuring the long-term viability of space activities and finding solutions to the problem of space debris.

The emergence of new technology is causing dramatic shifts to take place in practically every facet of our lives. From artificial intelligence and quantum computing to biotechnology and renewable energy, these discoveries provide potential for advancement and innovation that have never been seen before. On the other hand, they also bring with them complications concerning issues of ethics, security, privacy, and legislation. It is vital to strike a balance between innovative and responsible development and to approach these problems in a proactive manner if one want to make full use of the promise offered by emerging technology. The potential for the future of emerging technologies are very exciting; yet, the effective integration of these technologies into society will depend on our ability to manage the intricacies of these technologies and guarantee that everyone can benefit from them.

6.3 Envisioning the Role of Green Computing

The term "green computing," which can also be referred to as "sustainable computing" or "eco-friendly computing," refers to a notion that aims to reduce the negative effects that computing systems and practices have on the surrounding environment. Green computing plays an increasingly important role in reducing the carbon footprint left by the information technology industry as the world struggles to cope with the effects of climate change and the degradation of the environment. In this piece, we will investigate the multidimensional role that green computing plays in the context of a sustainable future, with a focus on the significance of green computing, the issues it faces, and the potential solutions to those challenges.

1. **The Importance of Environmentally Responsible Computing:**
   Reducing Our Impact on the Environment:
   The information technology industry is a large contributor to both electronic waste and emissions that contribute to climate change. The practice of green computing seeks to reduce energy consumption, limit electronic waste, and embrace sustainable practices in order to contribute to global efforts to battle climate change and protect the environment. e-waste minimization is another goal of green computing.
   Savings on Costs:
   Computing in an environmentally responsible manner can result in significant cost savings for businesses. Companies have the ability to cut their operational expenses and increase their profitability by optimizing their use of energy, prolonging the lifespan of their hardware, and minimizing waste.
   Conservation of Useable Resources:
   The practice of green computing promotes the responsible use of natural resources by encouraging the use of energy-efficient hardware, sustainable procurement, and activities that are favorable to the environment. This contributes to the conservation of resources and lessens the impact that technology has on the environment.
   Reputation in the Business World:
   Adopting environmentally friendly computing practices can boost a company's reputation and broaden its appeal to consumers who are concerned about the environment. Additionally, it might be a competitive advantage in a market that is becoming increasingly driven by concerns regarding sustainability.

Compliance with the Legislation:
Regulatory measures and financial incentives have been implemented in a number of nations to promote environmentally responsible computer operations. Not only is it necessary to comply with these requirements from a legal standpoint, but doing so is also helpful for the long-term viability of a corporation.

2. **Important Aspects of Eco-Friendly Computing:**
Efficiency in the Use of Energy:
Enhancing the energy efficiency of computer systems, such as personal devices, servers, and data centers, is at the core of green computing. Utilizing hardware that is efficient with energy, putting in place power-saving measures, and improving software are all necessary steps in this process.

Management of Electronic Waste:
It is necessary to dispose of electronic waste in a responsible manner and recycle it if one want to stop hazardous items from being dumped in landfills. Recycling and repairing of older technology are both encouraged by green computing practices.

Conservation of Useable Resources:
Reducing resource consumption as much as possible through the use of hardware consolidation, virtualization, and cloud computing can assist in lowering the demand for energy-intensive manufacturing processes and raw materials.

Sustainable Purchasing Practices:
During the purchasing process, organizations are strongly encouraged to select environmentally friendly components and materials whenever possible. Among these are the selection of products that have been awarded reputable environmental certifications.

Education and a Consciousness of the Facts:
It is essential, in order to cultivate a culture of sustainability within businesses and among individuals, to raise awareness of

environmentally responsible computing practices and to provide education on those practices.

3. **Obstacles to the Implementation of Eco-Friendly Computing:**
   Costs Incurred Upon Initial Investment:
   It is typically necessary to make early investments in energy-efficient hardware, software improvements, and personnel training in order to put green computing practices into effect. There may be reluctance on the part of certain organizations to invest resources for these reforms.
   Systems Left Behind:
   There are a lot of companies out there with legacy systems that are difficult to modernize or replace because they waste a lot of energy. Problems with compatibility and the expenses involved with upgrading can represent substantial roadblocks.
   Opposition to the Process of Change:
   The aversion to change that humans exhibit is a common barrier to the adoption of environmentally friendly computer methods. There is a possibility that workers will be hesitant to change their routines or to accept new technologies and workflows.
   Insufficient Awareness:
   There is still a sizeable section of the public that is oblivious of the effects that their computing behaviors have on the surrounding environment. The most important problem is to raise awareness about environmentally responsible computing.
   Obstacles Presented by Regulators:
   The absence of rules that are either consistent or stringent regarding the disposal of electronic waste and energy consumption can be a barrier for firms who want to embrace green computing practices.

4. **Alternatives and Methods for the Promotion of Eco-Friendly Computing:**
   There are a variety of approaches that may be taken to address these difficulties and increase the use of environmentally

responsible computing practices.

Solutions That Are More Economical:

Green computing solutions that are also cost effective should be given priority by organizations. Despite the fact that early investments may be necessary, they frequently result in cost savings over the longer term due to decreased energy usage and increased lifespans of equipment.

Understanding and Instruction:

To educate employees and individuals about the environmental impact of computing habits, awareness campaigns and training programs should be launched and provided respectively. Place an emphasis on the money you'll save as well as the other benefits of eco-friendly computing.

Incentive programs and regulatory frameworks:

To encourage the use of environmentally friendly computer practices, governments may offer financial incentives, tax benefits, or subsides. In addition, the implementation and enforcement of legislation relating to the disposal of electronic waste and the efficiency with which energy is used can help establish a more fair playing field.

Upgrades for Legacy Systems :

Provide companies with the financial help or incentives they need to upgrade or replace their outdated systems with alternatives that are more energy efficient. It is important to emphasize the long-term benefits as well as the return on investment (ROI) that these enhancements will provide.

Showcase Some Examples of Your Achievements:

Please provide any case studies or stories of triumph from companies that have effectively
adopted environmentally responsible computing practices. Examples taken from real life can both serve as a source of creativity and as validation of a notion.

Working Together and Forming Partnerships:

Encourage collaboration between governmental bodies, influential businesspeople, environmental organizations, and educational establishments. These alliances have the potential to accelerate research, development, and implementation of environmentally friendly computing technologies.

Sustainability Accreditations:

The use of environmentally friendly computer certifications and standards should be encouraged. These can act as standards for organizations who are working toward reducing their overall impact on the environment.

5. **The Part That Individuals Play in Environmentally Friendly Computing:**

The Conservation of Energy:

When not in use, turn off computers and other electronic devices, enable power-saving features, and utilize lighting that is as efficient as possible.

Disposal of Electronic Waste:

Recycling programs or responsible e-waste disposal services should be utilized in order to dispose of outdated electronic gadgets in an appropriate manner.

The Digital Minimalist Movement:

By eliminating superfluous files and emails, you can help free up storage space and lessen the requirement for new technology. This can be accomplished by decluttering your digital environment.

Sustainable Purchasing Practices:

When investing in new technology, make sure to look for energy-saving versions and brands that are dedicated to protecting the environment.

Effectiveness of Software:

Select software that makes effective use of available resources, and make it a habit to perform routine software and operating system updates in order to take advantage of enhancements that reduce energy use.

Work Done From Home:

When it is possible to do so, embrace remote work and telecommuting because doing so minimizes the demand for a real office space as well as the requirement to commute.

It is impossible to exaggerate how important environmentally responsible computing is to a sustainable future. It is not only the right thing to do from a moral standpoint, but also an absolute requirement in this ever-evolving world.

We can collectively lessen the environmental impact of the information technology sector by embracing energy-efficient hardware, encouraging responsible disposal of electronic waste, conserving resources, and increasing awareness about environmentally responsible computing activities. Adopting environmentally responsible practices in computers is crucial to preserving a healthy planet for future generations, as well as establishing a culture of sustainability and generating economic rewards. It is an essential move toward a more environmentally friendly and sustainable future.

Chapter 7

Tools, Resources, and Guidelines

In the world we live in today, which is always changing and moving at a breakneck rate, the pursuit of success frequently involves more than simply talent and ambition. It requires having access to the appropriate instruments, resources, and guidelines in order to traverse challenges, make decisions based on accurate information, and accomplish one's goals. This article covers a wide range of topics, including personal growth, business, education, and technology, and discusses a wide variety of tools, resources, and guidelines that can be applied in each of these areas. Individuals and organizations can improve their chances of succeeding in a global landscape that is becoming increasingly complicated and linked by gaining an awareness of these assets and making effective use of them.

1. **Growth and Development of the Self:**
1. **Instruments for Personal Evaluation:**
   Evaluations of Individual Characteristics:
   The Myers-Briggs Type Indicator (MBTI) and the Big Five Personality Traits are two examples of tools that can assist

individuals in gaining insights into their personalities, as well as their strengths and areas in which they can improve.

Identifying Your Strengths:

The StrengthsFinder evaluation developed by Gallup assists individuals in recognizing and capitalizing on their distinctive strengths, so enabling them to flourish in both their personal and professional life.

2. **Tools for Goal-Setting and Increasing Productivity:**
SMART Objectives:

The SMART criteria (Specific, Measurable, Achievable, Relevant, and Time-bound) offer a structured framework for effectively creating and attaining goals. These criteria stand for Specific, Measurable, Achievable, Relevant, and Time-bound.

Applications for the Management of Tasks and Projects:

Tools such as Trello, Asana, and Microsoft To-Do assist individuals in efficiently organizing their activities, determining their priorities, and managing their projects.

Techniques for Managing One's Time

Time management and productivity can both be improved with the use of certain methods, such as the Pomodoro Technique and the Eisenhower Matrix.

3. **Resources for Independent Improvement and Continuing Personal Development:**
Books and audiobooks, respectively:

Insights on personal growth can be gained from resources such as "The 7 Habits of Highly Effective People" by Stephen Covey and "Mindset" by Carol Dweck. Both of these authors have written books on the subject.

Webinars & Courses Offered Online:

Coursera, edX, and TED Talks are examples of online educational platforms that offer a diverse selection of lectures and classes pertaining to many aspects of personal growth.

Apps for Mental Health and Overall Well-Being:

Apps such as Calm, Headspace, and BetterHelp offer services to help users better manage stress and anxiety, as well as improve their mental health.

4. **Mentorship and Networking Opportunities:**

Websites Dedicated to Professional Networking:
Professional networking, the search for new employment, and the development of new skills can all be facilitated by platforms such as LinkedIn through the use of connections and groups.

Programming for Mentoring:
Individuals can take use of the chances provided by organizations and online mentorship platforms to interact with seasoned mentors for the purpose of gaining assistance and advancing their careers.

II. Commercial Activity and Business Entrepreneurship:

1. **The Planning and Strategy of the Business:**
   Examples of Business Plans: Templates
   Startups and entrepreneurs have access to free business plan templates and step-by-step instructions thanks to resources such as the Small Business Administration (SBA).
   The following is a SWOT analysis:
   Businesses can better evaluate the internal and external contexts in which they operate with the use of analytical techniques such as the SWOT analysis (which stands for strengths, weaknesses, opportunities, and threats).

2. **Management of the Financial Resources:**
   Software for Accounting Purposes
   Tools such as QuickBooks and Xero make it easier to handle finances, including creating budgets, issuing invoices, and keeping tabs on expenses.
   Instruction on Financial Matters:
   Educational sites such as Investopedia and Khan Academy

provide courses and articles on topics related to financial literacy and investment methods.

3. **Branding and Marketing Strategies:**
   Instruments for Managing Social Media:
   Platforms such as Hootsuite and Buffer make it possible for organizations to efficiently manage and schedule content for their social media accounts.
   Resources Available for Content Marketing:
   Producing and promoting marketing material is made easier with the assistance of content creation tools such as Canva and HubSpot's Blog Ideas Generator.
4. **Online Presence and Commercial Transactions:**

   Platforms for Electronic Commerce:
   Building and managing online stores is made easier with the help of comprehensive solutions provided by platforms such as Shopify and WooCommerce.
   Optimizing a website for search engines (SEO):
   Businesses may optimize their online presence and increase their search engine rankings with the assistance of SEO tools such as Moz and SEMrush.

   III. Learning and Educational Opportunities:

1. **Learning Environments Hosted Online:**
   MOOCs stand for "massive open online courses":
   The ability to continue one's education throughout one's lifetime is made possible through online learning environments such as Coursera, edX, and Udemy.
   OER stands for open educational resources.
   Repositories of open educational resources (OER) such as OpenStax and MIT OpenCourseWare offer free educational resources to students as well as teachers.

2. **Instruments for Research and Reference:**
   Databases Used in Education:
   Access to academic databases such as JSTOR and PubMed is one of the many excellent research resources offered by libraries and other academic organizations.
3. **Instruments for Citation and Bibliography:**
   Managing citations and generating bibliographies for research papers and projects is made easier with the assistance of tools such as Zotero and EndNote.
   Learning Management Systems (LMS) comes in at number three.
   Moodle and Canvas respectively:
   LMS platforms such as Moodle and Canvas are used extensively by educational institutions for the management of online courses and the distribution of online content.
   It's called Google Classroom:
   Google Classroom is a technology that makes it easy for teachers to construct and administer online learning spaces.
4. **Instructional Apps and the Gamification of Education:**

   Khan Academy and Duolingo are two examples:
   Apps such as Khan Academy and Duolingo make studying interactive and interesting, especially in topics such as mathematics and language study.
   Games Designed to Teach:
   The use of gamification platforms such as Kahoot! and Quizlet can turn educational activities into exciting and competitive contests.

IV. Innovation and Technological Advancement:

1. **Resources for Coding and Product Development:**
   When it comes to developing software, resources such as Python, Java, and Visual Studio Code are absolutely necessary.
   Coding Environments Available Online:

Platforms such as GitHub and Stack Overflow provide forums and repositories that can be used for collaborative problem-solving and development.

2. **New and Upcoming Technologies**
   Tools Utilizing Artificial Intelligence (AI):
   Developers now have the ability to design artificial intelligence (AI) and machine learning (ML) apps thanks to tools such as TensorFlow and PyTorch.
   The Development of Blockchain:
   Blockchain development can be accomplished with the help of tools and frameworks provided by resources such as Ethereum and Hyperledger Fabric.

3. **Software with an Open Source License:**
   Linux and Apache, respectively
   The powering of servers and infrastructure all around the world comes from open-source software such as Linux and Apache.
   GIMP and LibreOffice are examples.
   Individuals and businesses can cut their expenses by using cost-free alternatives to proprietary software, such as the word processing and image editing capabilities of LibreOffice and GIMP, respectively.

4. **Technological Communities and News:**

   Websites that Cover Tech News:
   Websites such as TechCrunch and Wired are excellent resources for keeping up with the most recent technological developments and trends.
   Communities in Technology:
   Discussions and the exchange of knowledge are made possible for people interested in technology through the use of online forums such as Hacker News and r/technology on Reddit.

5. **A Healthy and Happy Lifestyle:**

1. **Mobile Applications for Diet and Exercise: MyFitnessPal and Fitbit are two examples.**
   People can keep track of their eating, activity, and overall health with the assistance of apps and wearable devices like MyFitnessPal and Fitbit.
   Applications for Meditation and Mindfulness:
   Users of apps like Headspace and Calm are led through meditation and other exercises
   designed to relieve stress.
2. **Healthcare and Medical Resources: Resources for Healthcare**

   Comparing Mayo Clinic with WebMD:
   Websites such as WebMD and the Mayo Clinic provide individuals as well as those working in the medical field with access to reputable health information and resources.
   Providers of Telehealth Services
   Platforms for telehealth such as Teladoc give medical consultations and other healthcare services to patients remotely.

   VI. The Environment and Sustainable Development:

1. **Calculators for Environmental Impact:**
   Calculators of One's Carbon Footprint:
   The Carbon Footprint Calculator provided by the Carbon Trust is one tool that helps individuals and organizations evaluate the impact they have on the environment.
   Evaluations of the Energy Efficiencies:
   Assessments are offered to increase the energy efficiency of homes and businesses and are provided through services such as Energy Star.
2. **Education and Advocacy Concerning the Environment:**

   Organizations Concerned With the Environment:

Information and possibilities for environmental activism are made available through non-governmental organizations (NGOs) such as the World Wildlife Fund (WWF) and Greenpeace.

Platforms for Climate-Related Action:

Climate advocacy and awareness are promoted through the use of platforms such as the Climate Action Network (CAN) of the United Nations.

7. Legal and regulatory compliance

1. **Legal Investigation and Available Resources:**
   Databases Concerning Law:
   Access to legal statutes, rules, and case law can be obtained through the use of legal research databases such as LexisNexis and Westlaw.
   Templates & Forms for Legal Matters:
   Legal document templates and instruction are provided by a number of online services, including LegalZoom and Rocket Lawyer.
2. **Instruments for Compliance and Regulatory Affairs:**

   Software that ensures compliance:
   ComplyAdvantage and Thomson Reuters Regulatory Intelligence are two examples of software that can aid firms in meeting regulatory requirements and minimizing their exposure to legal risk.
   Compliance Resources with the GDPR:
   For help on complying with data protection and privacy standards, consult resources such as the website for the General Data Protection Regulation (GDPR) of the European Union.

VIII. Diversity and Inclusion

1. **Education Concerning Diversity and Inclusion:**
   Programs of Instruction:
   Training programs and materials pertaining to diversity and

inclusion can be found through organizations such as DiversityEdu and Catalyst.

Evaluations of Implicit Bias:
People are able to evaluate and address their unconscious prejudices with the assistance of tools such as the Harvard Implicit Bias Test.

2. **Recruitment and Hiring Practices That Promote Diversity**

Job Boards That Promote Diversity:
Websites such as DiversityJobs and INROADS connect candidates from varied backgrounds with companies that are committed to hiring a diverse workforce.

Job Descriptions That Include Everyone:
Textio and other such tools offer assistance on how to write inclusive job descriptions in order to attract a wide pool of applicants.

IX. **Participation in Social and Civic Activities:**

1. **Voting and Participation in Civic Life:**
Websites for the Registration of Voters:
Vote.gov and Rock the Vote are two examples of websites that provide resources and tools to encourage voter registration and civic participation.

Getting in Touch with Representatives:
Contacting elected representatives and engaging in civic action is made easier by platforms such as Resistbot and Countable.

2. **Resources for Volunteers and Nonprofit Organizations:**

Platforms for Volunteer-Based Partner Search:
Individuals can connect with local volunteer opportunities in their communities through the use of online platforms such as VolunteerMatch and Idealist.

Toolkits for Nonprofits:

Toolkits and other tools, such as the ones provided by the National Council of Nonprofits, are available for nonprofit organizations.

In the modern, fast-paced and interconnected world, the accessibility to tools, resources, and guidelines is one of the most important factors in terms of individual development, professional achievement, educational advancement, technological progress, and social advancement. Utilizing these assets gives individuals and organizations the strength to overcome obstacles, to make decisions based on accurate information, and to adapt to a landscape that is continuously changing. Individuals and organizations are able to manage complexity and plot a course toward a brighter and more prosperous future if they embrace a culture of continual learning and ingenuity. The vast array of tools and resources that are available in today's world provides an invaluable basis for success in the modern world, regardless of whether one is aiming to attain personal objectives, business objectives, educational accomplishments, or the impact one wishes to have on society.

7.1 Software Tools for Sustainable Development

The achievement of a sustainable development balance between economic expansion, the protection of the natural environment, and the improvement of social conditions is an essential global goal. Software solutions are becoming more relied upon by individuals and organizations alike in order to address the complex difficulties related with sustainability. These technologies facilitate the analysis of data, the making of decisions, the management of resources, and communication, ultimately leading to the promotion of behaviors that are ecologically responsible and socially equitable. In this piece, we will investigate a variety of software tools that, across a wide range of industries and fields, make a contribution to the advancement of sustainable development.

1. **Sustainability in regard to the Environment:**
1. **Methods of Environmental Supervision and Administration: Geographic Information Systems, or GIS for short:**
   Software for geographic information systems (GIS), such as

ArcGIS and QGIS, assists in the analysis of geographical data, which enables users to make more educated decisions regarding land use, conservation, and disaster management.

Instruments for Remote Sensing:

Environmental monitoring can be accomplished through the use of remote sensing software such as ENVI and Google Earth Engine, which allow for the collecting and analysis of satellite and aerial imagery.

2. **Management of carbon emissions and energy efficiency:**

   Systems for the Management of Energy

   Tracking and optimizing an organization's energy consumption can be made easier with the help of tools such as ENERGY STAR Portfolio Manager and EnerNOC.

   Calculators of One's Carbon Footprint:

   Carbon emissions can be calculated and reduced with the use of software like the Footprint Expert from Carbon Trust and the CoolClimate Calculator.

3. **Agriculture that is Sustainable:**

   Software Designed for Precision Agriculture:

   The application of data analytics on platforms such as FarmLogs and AgriTask allows for the optimization of farming techniques, the reduction of resource use, and the improvement in crop yields.

   Agricultural Simulation and Prognostication:

   The modeling of crops and the forecasting of agricultural outcomes are both helped tremendously by software tools such as DSSAT (Decision Support System for Agrotechnology Transfer).

   II. Concerning Social Equality:

   1. **Participation in the Community:**

      Tools for Social Media and Community Engagement:

      Platforms such as Hootsuite and Buffer facilitate organizations' engagement with communities, collection of feedback, and promotion of social projects.

Mapping of the Community:

Community mapping is made possible because to software such as Ushahidi and Community Analyst, which also enables participatory development and catastrophe response.

2. **Education and the Strengthening of Capabilities:**

Platforms for Electronic Learning:

Accessible education and training resources are made available by platforms such as Moodle
and edX, helping to close the knowledge gap in underserved regions.

Applications for the Study of Languages:

Apps like Duolingo and Rosetta Stone encourage language learning, which in turn helps to improve communication and fosters a more inclusive environment.

III. **The Development of the Economy:**

Microfinance and the Expansion of Financial Opportunities:

Application Software for Microfinance:

Microfinance organizations are able to provide financial services to underrepresented groups thanks to the availability of tools such as Mifos and Fineract.

Options for Making Digital Payments:

M-Pesa and PayPal are only two examples of mobile payment services that make it easier to conduct financial transactions in parts of the world where traditional banking is not widely available.

B. **An Analysis of Businesses and the Economy:**

Instruments for Economic Modeling:

Software programs such as IMPLAN and REMI assist enterprises and governments in determining the extent to which particular initiatives and policies will affect the economy.

Software for Conducting Market Research:

Market research, encouraging entrepreneurial activity, and making educated business decisions are all supported by tools such as SurveyMonkey and Qualtrics.

IV. Medical Care and General Health:

1. **Management of Healthcare Facilities:**
   Electronic Health Record Systems (often abbreviated as EHR):
   EHR software, such as Epic and Cerner, streamlines the management of healthcare data, which in turn reduces the amount of wasted paper and improves patient care.
   The Platforms for Telemedicine:
   Telehealth tools such as Zoom and Doxy.me provide remote healthcare services, which increases access to medical treatment while also lowering the requirement to travel.

2. **Monitoring of the Public Health System:**

   Software for Epidemiological Studies:
   The monitoring of diseases and the establishment of early warning systems are both facilitated by applications such as EpiInfo and HealthMap, which contribute to the conduct of public health actions.
   Systems for the Information of Patients' Health (HIS):
   In environments with limited access to resources, HIS software like DHIS2 and OpenMRS assists with the collecting and management of patient health data.

V. Community Development and Physical Facilities:

1. **Solutions for the Smart City:**
   Software for a Smart Grid:
   Tools such as Siemens Grid Diagnostic Suite improve the effectiveness of energy distribution and make it possible to more effectively control urban energy grids.
   Platforms for Urban Analytical Activities:

Simulation software like CityEngine and UrbanFootprint, for example, contributes to urban planning and sustainable development by modeling the expansion of cities and their underlying infrastructure.

2. **Management of the Public Transportation System:**

Software for Planning Transportation Systems:
The optimization of public transportation routes via tools such as TransCAD and PTV Visum helps cut down on traffic congestion and greenhouse gas emissions.

Ridesharing and mobile applications for mobility:
Mobility-sharing applications such as Uber and Lyft encourage carpooling and help minimize the number of private vehicles on the road.

VI. Preparation for Emergencies and Response to Crises:

1. **Instruments Used in Emergency Management:**
   The Application of GIS to Disaster Mapping:
   The use of GIS platforms allows for the creation of catastrophe risk maps as well as the
   evaluation of the impact of natural disasters.
   Systems for Notifying Residents of an Emergency:
   During times of emergency, software such as Everbridge and Alertus makes it possible to coordinate and send out large notifications.

2. **Aid and Relief to Humanitarian Crises:**

Management of the Supply Chain for Humanitarian Organizations:
During times of humanitarian crisis, using tools like the UNHRD's SMART and HUMLOG Planner can help make logistics and the distribution of resources more effective.

Mapping the Crisis and Using Crowdsourcing:

Platforms such as Ushahidi and Crisis Cleanup encourage the participation of volunteers and collect data in real time to assist with disaster relief efforts.

VII. Policy and Governance

1. **Openness and Transparency in Government:**
   Data Portals That Are Open:
   When governments publish datasets, they do so on publishing platforms such as Data.gov and Open Data Kit (ODK), which helps promote transparency and accountability.
   Application Software for Policy Analysis:
   Policymakers can better model and simulate the consequences of different policies with the use of modeling tools such as PolicyModel and NetLogo.
2. **Computerization of Government Procedures:**

   Solutions for Electronic Government:
   Automating administrative tasks using software like GovPilot and OpenGov leads to increased productivity and better quality of life for citizens.
   Administration of Voting and Elections:
   The use of election administration software helps to ensure that elections are both secure and transparent, which is beneficial to democratic governance.

When it comes to improving sustainability in all of its facets—economic, environmental, and social—the use of software tools has become very necessary. These technologies give individuals, businesses, and governments the ability to manage difficult situations, make decisions based on accurate information, and maximize the use of resources. The role that software tools play in the process of sustainable development is more important than it has ever been in a society that is struggling with environmental catastrophes, economic inequities, demands on healthcare, and urbanization. We can create a future that is more equal, beneficial to the environment, and wealthy for everyone if we make responsible use of technology and think creatively about how to apply it.

7.2 Key Organizations and Initiatives in Green Computing

The field of green computing has become of critical importance in this era, which is characterized by an increase in environmental concerns and the urgency to battle climate change. The goal of "green computing," also known as "sustainable computing" or "eco-friendly computing," is to lessen the negative effects that computer and information technology (IT) procedures have on the surrounding natural environment. This involves lowering the amount of energy that is used, as well as the trash produced by electronic devices, and implementing new technologies that are more environmentally friendly. The field of information technology has seen the emergence of a number of organizations and initiatives that are working to advance the field of green computing and advance more environmentally responsible business practices. In this piece, we will take a closer look at some of the most important groups and programs that are on the cutting edge of this revolutionary movement.

Green Electronics Council (abbreviated as GEC)

On a global scale, the advancement of environmentally friendly computing has been significantly aided by the non-profit organization known as the Green Electronics Council. The Global Electronics Council (GEC) was established in 2005 and is responsible for managing the Electronic Product Environmental Assessment Tool (EPEAT) program, which analyzes the impact that electronic devices have on the environment. Consumers and businesses who are looking for environmentally friendly electronics can benefit from EPEAT certification because it provides a trustworthy signal that assists them in making educated purchasing decisions.

The Environmental Protection Agency's (EPA) Energy Efficiency and Product Assessment Tool (EPEAT) evaluates items using a variety of criteria, including energy efficiency, material selection, and recyclability. The work that is done by the organization is not limited to only evaluating products; rather, it actively engages with manufacturers, government agencies, and non-governmental organizations (NGOs) to promote eco-design and green procurement practices in the electronics industry.

Energy Star

Energy Star is a well-known initiative that was first started by the Environmental Protection Agency (EPA) of the United States of America in the year 1992. It is primarily concerned with lowering the amount of energy used by electronic devices and home appliances. Products that are certified as energy-efficient by Energy Star are also regarded to be good to the environment. Consumers are able to discover products that spend less energy while keeping high performance requirements with the assistance of the Energy Star designation, which is recognized all over the world.

In addition to establishing standards for energy efficiency, Energy Star also carries out research and makes a variety of helpful information available to both individual customers and commercial enterprises. The initiative has been extended to cover a wider range of product categories, including commercial buildings and industrial facilities in addition to personal PCs and monitors.

The Grid in a Green Color

The Green Grid is an international organization that is comprised of both businesses and individuals that are committed to improving the energy efficiency of data centers and IT equipment. This firm was founded in 2007 with the goal of enhancing the environmental sustainability of data centers, which are infamous for the excessive amounts of energy that they consume. The Green Grid provides assistance to operators of data centers in lowering both their carbon footprint and their operational expenses by assisting in the development of best practices, guidelines, and benchmarks.

The Power Usage Effectiveness (PUE) measure is one of the most noteworthy contributions made by The Green Grid. This metric was developed to quantify the efficiency of data centers by comparing the amount of energy used for computation to the overall amount of energy consumed. Values of PUE that are lower indicate a higher degree of energy efficiency. This metric has been adopted as a standard in the data center sector, which has helped to spur competition as well as innovation in technology that save energy.

The Electronic Industry Citizenship Coalition, sometimes known as the "EICC"

The Electronic Industry Citizenship Coalition is now known as the Responsible Business Alliance (RBA), and it is a collaborative effort among the main corporations in the electronics industry to address issues of sustainability and social responsibility in the electronics supply chain. Despite the fact that its major focus is not only on environmentally friendly computing, it plays an important part in advancing sustainability within the electronic industry.

To encourage its member companies to lessen their negative effects on the environment, especially their carbon footprints, the EICC/RBA develops standards and codes of behavior for the companies in its membership. This includes making an attempt to reduce waste and energy usage as well as obtain materials in a responsible manner. The organization promotes environmentally responsible business practices throughout the entire electronic manufacturing process by establishing standards for the entire industry, as well as through encouraging transparency.

An Initiative to Save the Climate Through Computing

The Climate Savers Computing Initiative was started by Google and Intel in 2007 with the goal of lowering the amount of carbon that is produced by computing devices and data centers. The purpose of this program was to encourage enterprises to adopt greener information technology practices and to promote the use of energy-efficient computer systems. The development of more energy-efficient technology, improvements to power management, and the establishment of targets for reductions in data center energy use were among the primary aims.

The effort also worked with major IT companies to produce tools and resources for consumers and organizations to quantify their carbon emissions connected to computing and find ways to minimize them. These tools and resources can be found on this website. Even though the Climate Savers Computing Initiative came to an official close in 2010, the legacy it left behind continues to thrive in the form of increased knowledge and widespread adoption of energy-efficient computing methods.

EPSC stands for the Electronic Product Stewardship Council of Canada.

Electronic Product Stewardship Canada is a charitable organization based in Canada that is committed to the environmentally conscious management and recycling of electronic trash, sometimes known as "e-waste." EPSC plays a key role in the larger context of green computing by addressing the disposal and recycling of electronic equipment when they have reached the end of their lives. This is despite the fact that its primary focus is on electronic trash (e-waste).

The Electronics Product Stewardship Council (EPSC) collaborates closely with electronic

product makers, retailers, and other stakeholders to develop recycling programs and increase awareness about the significance of recycling electronic trash. EPSC helps to the reduction of the environmental impact that computing and IT equipment has by taking measures to ensure that electronic items are recycled and disposed of in an appropriate manner.

The Green Information and Technology Council.

The Green IT Council is an international organization with the mission of fostering sustainability and environmental responsibility within the information technology sector. It provides a variety of certifications and training programs for the purpose of educating IT professionals and companies on environmentally responsible computing practices. The Certified Green IT Professional (CGITP) certification is one of its most noteworthy projects. This certification verifies an individual's knowledge and skills in green information technology.

The Green IT Council is working to promote the use of energy-efficient technology, cut down on electronic waste, and reduce the amount of carbon dioxide that is produced as a result of IT operations through the advocacy and education initiatives that it is undertaking. The council helps to make the information technology industry more sustainable by providing IT professionals with the resources and the education they need to make decisions that are good for the environment.

SDIA stands for the Sustainable Digital Infrastructure Alliance.

The Sustainable Digital Infrastructure Alliance is a global organization with the mission of advancing environmentally responsible practices within the digital infrastructure industry. The term "digital infrastructure" refers to data centers, cloud computing, and various other essential elements of the information technology ecosystem. For the purpose of driving sustainability initiatives, SDIA brings together stakeholders from throughout the sector, including data center operators, cloud providers, and technology vendors.

The creation of industry standards and practices that are considered to be the finest for sustainable digital infrastructure is one of the primary goals of SDIA. This involves making an attempt to cut down on energy usage, improve the efficiency of operations in data centers, and make more use of renewable energy sources. Members of SDIA contribute to the creation of a digital infrastructure that is less harmful to the environment and uses less power by working together on sustainability initiatives.

Efforts and Projects Conducted Within Organizations

In addition to these well-known firms, other individual businesses as well as industry titans have made important strides in the development of environmentally friendly computing. As an illustration, Apple has made great strides toward lowering the environmental effect of both its products and the data centers that house them. The company's goal is to achieve carbon neutrality throughout the entirety of its supply chain and product lifecycle.

In a similar vein, Google has declared its intention to power its data centers and campuses solely with energy derived from renewable sources. Additionally, it has made a contribution to the creation of designs for servers that are more energy-efficient, such as the Open Compute Project. These projects are illustrative of the ever-increasing significance of environmental responsibility in the field of technology as well as the possibility for huge enterprises to be agents of constructive change.

Initiatives taken by respective governments

Directive on Ecologically Sound and Energy-Efficient Product Design of the European Union The European Union has passed regulations that require electronic items to meet specific energy efficiency and eco-design criteria. These laws contribute to a lessening of the negative effects that electronic products on the market in Europe have on the surrounding environment.

Green Government Information and Communications Technology Strategy (UK): The government of the United Kingdom has developed a Green Government Information and Communications Technology Strategy in an effort to lessen the impact that its IT operations have on the environment. This includes the promotion of the adoption of sustainable technology and the implementation of measures to increase energy efficiency in data centers.

Energy Efficiency projects (USA): In the United States, the federal government has begun a series of projects to increase the energy efficiency of federal data centers and to encourage the use of renewable energy sources in the operations of government information technology.

The term "green computing" is more than simply a passing fad; it actually refers to a significant movement with the overarching goal of reducing the negative effects that the information technology industry has on the natural world. Progression is being driven in this area by a number of important organizations and programs, including the Green

Electronics Council, Energy Star, The Green Grid, and a great number of others. These organizations are extremely important because of the critical role they play in establishing standards, advocating for environmentally responsible practices, and educating customers and businesses about the significance of environmentally responsible computing.

The necessity for environmentally responsible computer activities is becoming more apparent as the world's economy and society become more digitalized and dependent on technology. Individuals, businesses, and governments can all work together toward a more sustainable and ecologically responsible IT industry by providing support for the groups and programs listed above. This will, in the end, contribute to a greener future for our planet.

7.3 Practical Guidelines for Sustainable Software Practices

In today's world, sustainability has emerged as an issue of paramount importance, encompassing not just issues relating to the natural environment but also issues pertaining to society and the economy. When it comes to the creation of software, sustainability does not refer exclusively to the reduction of carbon footprints; rather, it refers to the production of software that is resilient, flourishes, and has a constructive effect on society. This article focuses on the environmental, social, and economic implications of sustainable software practices and outlines some practical guidelines for implementing those practices.

Before we begin:

The development of software can have a negative influence on the surrounding environment, hence sustainable software practices try to reduce this impact while also promoting social responsibility and ensuring long-term economic sustainability. When it comes to software development, achieving sustainability requires a number of interrelated strategies and practices. These strategies and practices can assist software engineers, teams, and organizations in aligning their efforts with broader societal and environmental goals.

Sustainability in Relation to the Environment

1. **Development of Eco-Friendly Software**
    Application development that is focused on conserving energy is known as "green software development." The developers of the application should think about optimizing the code and using algorithms that use fewer resources. In addition, reducing energy consumption and emissions of greenhouse gases can be accomplished by developing software that is capable of functioning well on low-power devices and in data centers.
2. **Optimizing the Use of Cloud Computing**
    Computing in the cloud has emerged as an essential component of today's modern software
    development. On the other hand, inefficient use of cloud resources might result in wasteful consumption of energy. Optimum cloud resource allocation, implementation of auto-scaling, and selection of environmentally responsible cloud service providers that make use of renewable energy sources are all examples of sustainable practices.
3. **Reduce the physical imprint of the data center**
    The consumption of electricity by data centers is significant. Consolidating servers, utilizing virtualization, and investigating co-location options are three ways to cut down on the amount of required physical space and increase the data center's energy efficiency. Using renewable energy sources and cooling systems that are efficient in their use of energy are both ways to further reduce the negative impact on the environment.
4. **Management of Software During Its Lifecycle**
    Throughout the whole lifecycle of the software, keep the influence on the environment in mind. Reducing waste, reusing code and components, and optimizing software updates to use as few resources as possible are all approaches that are part of sustainable software development.

The Duty to Care for Others

5. **The Development of Morally Sound Software**
   Ethical considerations ought to be put at the forefront of software development by both individual developers and organizations. This involves protecting the privacy of the user, preventing the use of potentially harmful algorithms, and ensuring that the software is accessible to all users, regardless of whether or not they have a disability.

6. **Embracing Difference and Promoting Inclusion**
   More inclusive software is the result of diverse team composition. Create an atmosphere at work that values the contributions of people from a variety of experiences and points of view. Enhancing software quality, promoting fairness, and ensuring that software serves a wider spectrum of users are all accomplished through the practice of inclusivity.

7. **Open Source Software and Working Together**
   Embrace open-source methods as a means of fostering collaboration and facilitating the exchange of information. When compared to proprietary solutions, open-source software typically has a bigger community of contributors and has the potential to evolve in a more sustainable manner. In addition, the use of open-source software can lessen dependence on a single provider and increase interoperability.

8. **Design with the User in Mind**
   User-centered design methods should be given priority in order to develop software that satisfies the requirements and expectations of users. Continuous feedback loops, iterative design methods, and usability testing help to ensure that software retains its relevance and value throughout time.
   Ability to survive economically

9. **An examination of the "Total Cost of Ownership" (TCO)**
   Sustainable software development approaches take into account the effect on the economy over the long run. Conduct an analysis of the total cost of ownership, which should include the costs

of both development and maintenance as well as operational expenses. This analysis assists in making educated judgments regarding the distribution of resources and investments.

10. **Capacity for Scale and Adaptability**
    Develop software that is flexible enough to meet changing requirements and is successful at scaling. Scalable software reduces the need for expensive rewrites or replacements, ensuring a longer lifespan and improved economic returns. Scalability also allows for greater flexibility in meeting changing business needs.
11. **The Management of Risk**
    Early on in the course of development, risks should be identified and efforts made to mitigate them. In order to avoid time-consuming and financially burdensome problems, sustainable software practices require proactive risk management.
12. **The Transfer of Knowledge**

Make an investment in the sharing of information within your firm. Ensure that best practices are documented, that thorough documentation is produced, and that members of the team are able to easily share their acquired knowledge with one another. This ensures that the software will be around for a long time and lessens the dependence on specialized individuals.Sustainable software practices are an all-encompassing method for the development of responsible software since they take into account not just environmental but also social and economic factors. Software developers, teams, and organizations may all make a contribution to a more sustainable future by following these rules and putting them into practice. Green software development, ethical considerations, and economic viability are all interconnected aspects of software sustainability that ought to be incorporated into software development processes from the very beginning. Sustainable software practices are a crucial step in addressing the world's complicated challenges and creating a beneficial impact not just on society but also on the environment. This is especially true as the globe continues to struggle with a variety of issues.

Chapter 8

Conclusion and Call to Action

It is impossible to exaggerate how vitally important sustainable practices are to the process of developing software in today's quickly advancing technological landscape. The environmental impact of software and the hardware infrastructure that supports it is the focus of the field of green computing, which is a subfield of sustainability. In this article, the important facets of green computing have been discussed, and the article has emphasized the significance of green computing in reducing the negative effects of the digital era on the environment. As we get to the end of this conversation, it is essential to consider the most important insights and issue a call to action for individuals, corporations, and the community of software developers to embrace and encourage green computing techniques.

A Review of Eco-Friendly Computing

Energy efficiency refers to the process of reducing the amount of power used by computing resources such as data centers, servers, and client devices by optimizing both hardware and software.

Resource conservation is the practice of managing computer resources such as storage, memory, and processing power in an effective manner in order to minimize waste and maximize the efficiency of the system as a whole.

E-waste reduction refers to the use of proper disposal and recycling techniques in order to lessen the amount of garbage generated by electronic devices and software that has become obsolete.

Transitioning to renewable energy sources, such as solar and wind power, to power data centers and other IT infrastructure is one aspect of the renewable energy movement.

Virtualization refers to the process of employing virtualization techniques in order to maximize the usage of available resources and minimize the requirement for actual hardware.

The creation of software programs that are resource-conscious, use energy efficiently, and are developed with long-term sustainability in mind is referred to as "green software development."

Accomplishments Made in the Field of Green Computing

1. **Data Centers That Are Efficient in Their Use of Energy**
   The commitments made by major technology corporations to power their data centers with energy derived from renewable sources would result in a considerable drop in the amount of greenhouse gases released into the atmosphere. The design of data centers and the cooling technologies they use have also undergone significant innovation, which has contributed to increased energy efficiency.

2. **Computing in the Virtual Cloud and Virtualization**
   Virtualization technologies have made it possible for businesses to consolidate their server infrastructure and maximize their use of available resources. Platforms for cloud computing provide solutions that are scalable as well as efficient in terms of energy use, which helps to eliminate the requirement for on-premises infrastructure.

3. **Practices for Eco-Friendly Software**
   The developers are becoming more conscious of the effects that

their work has on the environment. The widespread use of "green software practices," which include the optimization of source code and the development of efficient algorithms, has led to the creation of software that uses less resources and operates more effectively.

4. **Initiatives Regarding the Recycling of Electronics**

The expansion of consumer and commercial participation in environmentally responsible disposal and recycling programs has contributed to the growth of recycling efforts for electronic trash. Because of this, huge volumes of e-waste have been saved from being dumped in landfills.

The Critical Need for More Eco-Friendly Computing

Despite the fact that these accomplishments should be celebrated, the need for environmentally responsible computing has never been higher. The rise in demand for cloud services, the proliferation of digital technologies, and the expansion of the Internet of Things (IoT) have all contributed to an increase in the amount of energy that is consumed by information technology infrastructure. In particular, data centers continue to be voracious consumers of power, which contributes significantly to the production of carbon emissions.

In addition, the rapid speed of software development, which is characterized by frequent upgrades and short lifecycles, has the potential to generate a significant amount of e-waste if it is not carefully managed. In light of the environmental impacts that are caused by the disposal of hardware as well as the energy requirements associated with the execution of software, there is an urgent requirement for complete green computing techniques.

The Urgent Plea for Action

1. **People on their Own and Customers**
   Educate Yourself: Be aware of the effects that your digital activities have on the surrounding environment. Be aware of the

amount of energy that is being used by your gadgets and make decisions based on accurate information.

Recycle in a Responsible Manner: Old electronic equipment should be disposed of through the appropriate recycling procedures. Electronic garbage collection programs are offered by a variety of local recycling facilities and manufacturers.

Consider making purchases of energy-efficient and environmentally friendly technology to show your support for green technology. Keep an eye out for products that have been awarded the Energy Star accreditation and are made from environmentally friendly components.

Be a Champion for Change: Raise awareness about environmentally friendly computing activities and encourage your community to embrace sustainable technological habits.

2. **Corporations and other types of organizations**

    Embrace Renewable Energy: Make investments in sources of renewable energy to power your data centers and other components of your information technology infrastructure. Make a commitment to lowering the amount of carbon emissions that are caused by your business.

    Implementing energy-efficient data center designs, cooling systems, and server virtualization are all important steps in optimizing data centers. Maintain constant oversight and strive to enhance energy efficiency.

    The technique of selecting hardware and software vendors who place a priority on sustainability and environmentally friendly operations is known as "green procurement." Think about how long the product will last and whether it can be recycled.

    Green software development involves incentivizing developers of software to adopt "green coding" methods and placing an emphasis on energy efficiency in software architecture.

    Assessing and bettering the environmental effect of your entire

technology supply chain, from manufacturing to disposal, is an important step in creating a more sustainable supply chain.
3. **The Community for the Development of Software**

Software Developers Should Be Encouraged to Adopt Green Coding Practices Green coding practices should be encouraged among software developers. Incentivize the optimization of source code, the development of resource-conscious algorithms, and software architecture.

Open Source Collaboration: Embrace open-source software development, which frequently leads to solutions that are more sustainable and eco-friendly since they are driven by creativity from the community.

Advocate for software with longer lifecycles and support for older hardware in order to reduce the number of times that updates and replacements need to be performed. This is part of lifespan management.

Education and Awareness: Educate software engineers and programmers about the environmental impact of their work and the significance of using environmentally friendly computing practices.

Green Metrics: Create and use metrics to evaluate the effect that software applications have on the environment. These metrics should provide software developers with input on how they may improve their sustainability efforts.

The use of environmentally friendly computer technology is not merely a passing fad but rather an absolute prerequisite for the 21st century. The advent of the digital age has presented both previously unimaginable opportunities and difficulties, and our approach to overcoming these difficulties must be founded in sustainability.

We can pave the road for a more sustainable and responsible future if we acknowledge the environmental repercussions of software development and embrace methods that promote the use of environmentally friendly computing technologies.

Because of the severity of the climate catastrophe, collective action is required, and the community of software developers is in a position unlike any other to take the initiative. As we come to the end of our investigation into green computing, let us not forget that every single line of code, every single data center, and every single digital device all have a part in determining the influence that we have on the environment. We can lessen our impact on the environment, make better use of the resources we have, and create a digital world that will be more sustainable for future generations if we accept the principles of green computing and take concrete steps to implement them.

8.1 Recap of Key Takeaways

We have gone into the complicated web of environmental concerns, solutions, and the essential call to action in this extensive conversation on green computing and sustainability in software. This discussion covers topics such as green computing and sustainability in software. As we recall the most important lessons from this discussion, it is vital to pause and think about the critical insights and concrete recommendations that help steer individuals, corporations, and the community of software developers toward a more responsible and environmentally friendly future.

The Pressing Need to Achieve Sustainability

The pressing need to address environmental challenges, notably climate change, highlights the need of sustainability in all parts of life, including the creation of technology and software. This is due to the fact that there is an environmental imperative to do so.

The advent of digital technology has resulted in an explosion in the amount of data and energy that is being consumed. As a result, it is more important than ever to take into account the effects that our digital actions will have on the natural world.

Emissions of Carbon: Data centers, a linchpin of the digital age, are substantial contributors to carbon emissions, highlighting the significance of lowering the energy usage of these facilities.

E-Waste Problem: The quick obsolescence of software combined with the proliferation of electronic devices has led to a growing e-waste problem, which in turn necessitates the implementation of responsible disposal and recycling measures.

The Basics of Environmentally Friendly Computing

Energy Efficiency: One of the most important aspects of environmentally friendly computing is energy efficiency. It is absolutely necessary to optimize the hardware and software used in data centers, servers, and client devices in order to reduce the amount of energy consumed by these components.

Conservation of resources: An effective management of computing resources, such as storage, memory, and processing power, leads to a reduction in waste and an improvement in the overall performance of the system.

Reducing E-waste: Disposal and recycling procedures that are responsible assist reduce the amount of electronic trash that is generated by outdated hardware and software.

Energy from Renewable Sources One of the most important strategies for lowering the carbon footprint of computers is making the switch to powering data centers and IT infrastructure with energy from renewable sources.

Virtualization: Technologies that enable virtualization maximize the use of available resources while simultaneously lowering the requirement for actual hardware. This results in significant energy savings.

Green software development is an essential component of green computing since it involves the creation of software programs that minimize the use of resources, conserve energy, and are developed with sustainability in mind.

Accomplishments and Forward Progress

Data Centers That Are Efficient in Their Use of Energy Many of the most successful organizations in the technology sector have made a commitment to powering their data centers with renewable energy sources, which has led to significant reductions in carbon emissions.

Virtualization and Cloud Computing Virtualization methods and cloud computing platforms offer scalable and energy-efficient solutions that decrease the requirement for on-premises infrastructure. These solutions are offered via virtualization.

Green Software Development Methods Developers are becoming more aware of the impact that software has on the environment, which has led to the development of green software development methods and more efficient software design.

Initiatives for Electronic Recycling: There has been an increase in the number of responsible disposal and recycling programs, which has resulted in the diversion of a substantial volume of e-waste away from landfills.

An Appeal to Take Action

Individual Responsibilities: Individuals can make a difference by understanding and reducing the environmental impact of their digital habits, recycling electronic gadgets, and supporting green technology options. Individuals can also choose to support environmentally friendly technologies.

The adoption of renewable energy sources, the optimization of data centers, the practice of green procurement, and the prioritization of green software development are all business commitments that can help organizations lessen their impact on the environment.

Software Development Community: The software development community plays an essential part in the promotion of green coding methods, open-source collaboration, lifecycle management, education and awareness, as well as the development of green metrics.

This takes a more holistic approach.

Interconnected Aspects Green computing is a comprehensive strategy that includes energy efficiency, resource conservation, e-waste reduction, renewable energy, virtualization, and green software practices. This holistic approach was developed to reduce the environmental impact of computing. These aspects are inextricably linked to one another and support one another.

Long-Term Thinking: In order for software and technology to be sustainable, one must adopt a long-term perspective that takes into account the lifecycle of both hardware and software. The goal of this perspective is to lengthen the amount of time that these components may be used and to decrease the number of replacements that are required.

Responsibility on a Collective Scale: Achieving sustainability in software is a group effort that calls for the active participation of individuals, businesses, governments, and the community of software developers. The importance of working together and taking on responsibilities jointly cannot be overstated.

How We Can Move Forward

Innovation Perpetual: The quest of environmentally friendly computing and sustainability in software calls for perpetual innovation and adaptation to the development of new technologies and the emergence of new environmental concerns.

Education and Awareness It is vital, in order to cultivate a culture of sustainability, to educate individuals and organizations about the environmental impact of digital technology as well as to increase environmental awareness among the general public.

Advocacy and Policy It is essential, in order to bring about systemic change, to advocate for rules and regulations that encourage sustainable computing practices and sustainable computing best practices.

The development of measures and benchmarks to quantify the impact that software applications have on the environment, as well as the ongoing improvement of sustainability efforts, are both essential to the forward movement of the industry.

8.2 The Importance of Individual and Collective Action

It is impossible to overestimate the significance of individual and group action in a world that is struggling to overcome challenges that are both interconnected and complex. Whether people or groups are addressing global challenges such as climate change, social injustice, or public health crises, or more localized concerns, the activities of individuals and groups have a significant impact on the present and future of our communities. This piece examines the relevance of individual as well as group action, stressing the complimentary roles that each plays in bringing about positive change and sculpting a better society.

The Influence That Individual Action Can Have

1. Individual Accountability: The activities of a single person are what ultimately bring about change in a society. Making responsible decisions that are beneficial to society as a whole is something that everyone is responsible for doing. Personal responsibility can be embodied in a variety of acts taken by an individual, such as minimizing one's own carbon impact or advocating for a more ethical consumer culture.
2. Being a Catalyst for Change The annals of history are full with tales of individuals who were the catalysts for revolutionary change. Greta Thunberg, Mahatma Gandhi, and Martin Luther King Jr. are just a few examples of forward-thinking individuals who have shown that a single person's commitment to a cause and unwavering belief can change the trajectory of history.
3. By modeling positive behaviors, individuals motivate those around them to do the same, which is the third and last step in the setting of examples process. For instance, incorporating environmentally responsible behaviors into one's day-to-day life, such as recycling or energy conservation, might encourage one's friends, family, and coworkers to do the same.
4. Leveraging abilities and experience Individuals possess one-of-a-kind abilities, talents, and experience that can be directed toward the solution of particular problems if the appropriate opportunities are taken advantage of. Individuals are able to make important contributions based on their abilities, whether it be through the act of volunteering, the exchange of knowledge, or the invention of novel solutions.
5. Advocacy and Increasing Awareness: When it comes to lobbying for change, the voices of individuals matter. Individuals now have access to strong tools that can help them raise awareness about important causes, generate support, and mobilize communities thanks to the proliferation of social media and digital platforms.

The Power that Comes from Working Together

1. Amplification of influence: Although the effects of individual activities are significant, the influence of collective efforts can be multiplied by a factor of ten or more. When people come together in support of a similar goal, the collective efforts of those individuals have the potential to affect change on a wider scale.
2. The Pooling of Resources: Collective action makes it possible to combine a variety of resources, including financial, human, and intellectual assets. The mobilization of these resources makes it possible to support research, begin campaigns, and provide assistance to individuals who are in need.
3. The ability to influence political decisions by collective action, which can also hold governments and companies accountable for their actions. The strength of collective advocacy has been shown by movements such as the fight for civil rights, the right of women to vote, and the fight for environmental protection.
4. A Sense of Shared duty: Participating in a group effort helps to instill a sense of shared duty and encourages community involvement. It fosters a sense of connection and purpose in its participants by encouraging group efforts directed toward the achievement of shared objectives.
5. Sustainability: In order to solve many problems, including climate change and the deterioration of the environment, it will be necessary to make systemic reforms. Individual activities will not be sufficient. The institutions are forced to make these adjustments as a result of the pressure that is applied by collective action.

8.3 The Role of Green Computing in a Sustainable Future
Technology plays an essential part in both our day-to-day lives and the functioning of the economy on a global scale in the increasingly digital world of today. Nevertheless, there is an environmental cost associated with the proliferation of digital devices and data centers. The

information technology industry is a major contributor to the production of greenhouse gases, the disposal of electronic waste, and the consumption of energy. The concept of "green computing" has arisen as a vital component of environmental stewardship and responsible technology development in order to solve these difficulties and work towards a more sustainable future. Green computing combines the concepts of "computer" and "environment." In this essay, we will investigate the function that "green computing" plays in promoting sustainability and reducing the negative effects of the information technology industry on the natural environment.

Comprehending the Concept of Green Computing

The concept of "green computing," which is also known as "sustainable IT" or "eco-friendly computing," refers to the process of developing, manufacturing, utilizing, and disposing of computing resources in an environmentally responsible manner. Other names for "green computing" include "sustainable IT" and "eco-friendly computing." It includes a wide variety of approaches and guiding ideas with the goal of lowering the negative effects that information technology has on the surrounding environment. The basic goals of green computing are to reduce the amount of energy that is consumed, the amount of electronic waste that is produced, and the amount of carbon footprint that is associated with IT operations.

Effective Use of Energy

An essential component of environmentally friendly computing is energy efficiency. Data centers are notoriously wasteful when it comes to energy use because they hold the servers and infrastructure that power our digital world. It takes a startling amount of electricity to keep these facilities operating and at a comfortable temperature. The amount of electricity that data centers can use has been estimated to be comparable to that of small cities. Green computing encourages the use of hardware and software solutions that have a lower impact on the environment and consume less energy in order to solve this problem.

The production of energy-efficient hardware components, like as CPUs, memory, and storage devices, has advanced significantly thanks to the efforts of hardware manufacturers. These components have been developed to have a lower power consumption while maintaining or even improving their overall performance. In addition, the development of cooling systems that are more efficient and the exploitation of renewable energy sources have further contributed to the reduction of the environmental impact that data centers have.

Green computing encourages the use of energy-efficient software designs and algorithms, particularly in the software sector of the industry. This comprises optimizing the code to limit the amount of CPU and memory that is used, minimizing the amount of energy that is consumed by programs, and implementing strategies for power management to guarantee that devices enter low-power modes when they are not being used.

Reduce Your Use Of Electronic Waste

The lightning-fast pace at which technological progress is being made has directly contributed to the explosion in the number of electronic devices. The accumulation of electronic waste, sometimes known as e-waste, is an increasing concern as older electronic gadgets are rendered obsolete. If it is not correctly managed, electronic trash can provide significant dangers to both the environment and human health because it contains toxic components. Green computing is an approach that aims to solve this problem by encouraging disposal procedures that are environmentally friendly and actions that lengthen the lifespan of computing equipment.

Adopting modular and upgradable hardware designs is one strategy for reducing the amount of electronic waste produced. This gives customers the ability to repair or upgrade particular components, like as RAM or storage, rather of having to throw away the entire device every time an upgrade is required. Additionally, vital components of green computing include recycling programs and activities that promote the refurbishing and reuse of outdated electronic equipment.

Responsible Methods in the Administration of Information Technology

The term "green computing" refers to the use of environmentally friendly methods in all elements of information technology, including but not limited to hardware and software. This includes technologies such as virtualization, cloud computing, and remote work, all of which have the potential to drastically lower an organization's overall carbon footprint.

The practice of operating several virtual machines on a single physical server is known as virtualization. This helps to maximize the use of available resources while simultaneously minimizing the number of actual servers that are needed. Not only does this help save energy, but it also decreases the amount of actual space that is required for data centers.

Through the use of cloud computing, businesses are able to delegate their data processing and storage requirements to remote data centers run by cloud service providers. These providers frequently implement cutting-edge energy-efficient technology and processes, which enables enterprises to cut down on the amount of on-premises infrastructure they use and the amount of energy they consume.

The concept of remote work, which gained popularity during the COVID-19 pandemic, has the ability to lower the carbon footprint that is involved with commuting as well as the amount of energy that is consumed in the office. By giving workers the option to perform their jobs from their homes or other off-site locations, companies can cut down on the amount of office space they use and the amount of energy they consume as a result.

The Economic Argument in Favor of Eco-Friendly Computing

Although environmental concerns are the primary impetus behind green computing, there is a compelling commercial argument to be made for implementing environmentally friendly practices in the information technology sector. It is possible for sustainable IT initiatives to result in cost reductions, improvements in business reputation, and increases in competitiveness.

Reduced Expenditures

The possibility of monetary savings presents businesses with one of the most compelling reasons to embrace environmentally responsible computing: becoming green. Hardware and data center designs that are more energy-efficient have the potential to result in cheaper electricity bills and reduced operational expenses. For instance, the implementation of server virtualization can result in greater utilization of available resources, which in turn reduces the requirement for more servers and brings down overall energy usage.

In addition, it is possible to lower the amount of money spent on capital expenditures for the replacement of computer equipment by prolonging the lifespan of that equipment using modular designs and ethical disposal methods. It is possible for businesses to lessen their negative impact on the environment while simultaneously improving their bottom line if they make investments in energy-efficient equipment and processes.

Reputation of the Business

Consumers and other stakeholders are becoming more aware of environmental challenges, and as a result, they frequently give preferential treatment to businesses that can demonstrate a commitment to sustainability. Businesses that use environmentally friendly computing methods can improve their company reputation and attract clients who are concerned about the environment. This positive image has the potential to convert into improved consumer loyalty as well as value for the business.

In addition, numerous national governments and regulatory agencies are working to enact rules that either encourage or mandate the reduction of carbon emissions and other negative environmental impacts caused by corporations. Businesses have a better chance of being in compliance with existing as well as upcoming environmental standards if they take proactive steps to embrace environmentally friendly computing practices.

Innovation and Competitivity in Business

The concept of "green computing" places an emphasis on innovation. Businesses that make investments in research and development to develop technology that consume less energy and sustainable IT solutions might gain a competitive advantage in the marketplace. They have the ability to design goods and services that can meet the rising demand for environmentally friendly technologies, hence creating new opportunities in the market.

In addition, within the community of environmentally conscious computer users, collaboration and the exchange of information are key drivers of innovation and the creation of cutting-edge technologies. Organizations are able to retain their level of competitiveness and continue to be on the cutting edge of technological breakthroughs when they take part in a collaborative ecosystem like this one.

The Obstacles in Our Way and the Way Forward

While there has been substantial progress achieved in the adoption of environmentally friendly

computing techniques, there are still a number of difficulties and possibilities that lie ahead on the path towards a more sustainable IT industry.

Energy Supply Options

The supply of energy that is utilized to power IT infrastructure is one of the most significant obstacles that must be overcome in green computing. Even while many data centers have already made the switch to renewable energy sources, there are still many areas that primarily rely on fossil fuels for the generation of electricity. It is vital, in order to reduce the carbon footprint of the information technology industry, to ensure access to clean, renewable energy.

Management of Electronic Waste

The effective management of electronic trash is still a key obstacle to overcome. Even though there have been efforts made to recycle and rehabilitate electronic waste, there is still a significant quantity of material that is improperly disposed of or ends up in landfills. This poses concerns to both the environment and human health. To find a solution to this problem, the recycling infrastructure needs to be upgraded, and there needs to be a more thorough collection program for electronic waste.

Privacy and protection of sensitive data

Data privacy and security issues are becoming an increasingly pressing worry for businesses as cloud computing and other forms of remote work grow increasingly prevalent. It is a difficult issue to strike a balance between the requirements for safe data management and the low energy consumption of cloud-based services. To successfully manage this balance, further improvements in cloud computing that are both secure and efficient will be required.

Both the Plan and the Rules

The adoption of environmentally friendly computing methods can be strongly impacted by the rules and regulations enacted by governments. The promotion of ecologically responsible technology development and consumption through the use of incentives, tax breaks, and penalties for non-compliance are all potential tactics that could prove to be effective. It is absolutely necessary for policymakers to work together with various industry stakeholders in order to produce policies that are well-informed and efficient.

Education and a Consciousness Campaign

It is vital to educate consumers, organizations, and IT professionals about the significance of environmentally responsible computing in order to accelerate adoption. Educating the IT community about environmentally responsible practices through awareness campaigns, training programs, and certifications can assist the IT community become more environmentally conscientious.

Computing that is less harmful to the environment is an essential component of a more sustainable future. It is imperative that steps be taken to mitigate the environmental impact of the information technology industry as technology continues to play an ever more significant part in our everyday lives. Green computing offers a way toward a more ecologically responsible and commercially successful information technology business by increasing energy efficiency, decreasing electronic waste, and applying sustainable practices. This can be accomplished through green computing. The adoption of environmentally friendly computing practices is not only a moral need, but also a competitive advantage for businesses that wish to flourish in an era in which a commitment to sustainability is a primary factor in determining levels of success. We can work together, foster innovation, and make a commitment to the responsible development of technology in order to get closer to a future in which technology improves the quality of our lives while also protecting the integrity of our planet.

www.ingramcontent.com/pod-product-compliance
Lightning Source LLC
LaVergne TN
LVHW011938070526
838202LV00054B/4718